The

Reminiscences of

Captain Willard G. TRIEST, CEC, USNR (Ret.)

U. S. Naval Institute
Annapolis, Maryland

1977

Preface

This volume contains the transcript of six taped interviews with Captain Willard G. Triest, CEC, USNR (Ret.) at his office in Annapolis, Maryland during the summer of 1972. They were obtained by John T. Mason, Jr. for the Oral History program of the U. S. Naval Institute.

Captain Triest has reviewed and corrected the text. It has been re-typed, and indexed before binding. An appendix is included at the end of the volume. Captain Triest has made available a number of photographs. They have been inserted at the place in the text where they are most valuable as illustrations.

This is an exceedingly interesting memoir. It begins with the formative period of the SeaBees in World War II. Captain Triest has an engaging narrative style and describes most graphically the activities of his 27th Battalion of SeaBees on Tulagi-Guadalcanal, Emirau, and Okinawa. In telling his story the Captain actually provides another dimension to the growing collection of memoirs, covering the war in the Pacific.

John T. Mason, Jr.
Director of Oral History
U. S. Naval Institute

TABLE OF CONTENTS

		Page
Chapter I -	Quonset Point Naval Air Station, R.I.	1
	Naval Construction Training Center, Davisville, R.I.	
	Lend-Lease Operations:	
	Atlantic - Iceland, Ireland, Scotland, Azores	
	Pacific - Bora Bora Island - beginning of the Seabees.	
Chapter II -	Preparation for overseas assignment.	49
	57th Naval Construction Battalion - Lion I.	
	Espiritu Santo, New Hebrides, Pacific.	
	27th NCB - Tulagi.	
Chapter III -	Guadalcanal, Solomons Islands	106
	Auckland, New Zealand	
	Pontoon bridges	
	Emirau Island.	
Chapter IV -	Return to Camp Parks, California for refit.	156
	Story of two year experiences written - "Meat On The Table."	
Chapter V -	Okinawa, Ryukyuan Islands	
	Visits to Tokoyo, Japan - Chosen, Korea.	
Chapter VI -	Okinawa	220
	Military Role	
	Resettlement of natives - Ryukyuans	
	War ends.	

DECLARATION OF TRUST

The undersigned does hereby appoint and designate as his (her) Trustee herein, the Secretary-Treasurer and Publisher of the United States Naval Institute to perform and discharge the following duties, powers, and privileges in connection with the possession and use of a certain taped interview between the undersigned and the Oral History Department of the United States Naval Institute.

1. Classification of Transcript.

    (✓)a. If classified OPEN, the transcript(s) may be read or the recording(s) audited by the qualified personnel upon presentation of proper credentials, as determined by the Secretary-Treasurer of the U.S. Naval Institute.

    ( )b. If classified PERMISSION REQUIRED TO CITE OR QUOTE, the user will be required to obtain permission in writing from the interviewee prior to quoting or citing from either the transcript(s) or the recording(s).

    ( )c. If classified PERMISSION REQUIRED, permission must be obtained in writing from the interviewee before the transcribed interview(s) can be examined or the tape recording(s) audited.

    ( )d. If classified CLOSED, the transcribed interview(s) and the tape recording(s) will be sealed until a time specified by the interviewee. This may be until the death of the interviewee or for any specified number of years.

2. It is expressly understood that in giving this authorization, I am in no way precluded from placing such restrictions as I may desire upon use of the interview at any time during my lifetime, nor does this authorization in any way affect my rights to the copyright of my literary expressions that may be contained in the interview.

Witness my hand and seal this 16 day of Sept 1977

[signature]

I hereby accept and consent to the foregoing Declaration of Trust and the powers therein conferred upon me as Trustee:

[signature: R H E Bowker Jr]

Triest #1 - 1

Interview #1 with Captain Willard G. Triest, CEC, USNR
(Retired)

Place: Annapolis, Maryland

Date: Thursday morning, 6 July 1972

Subject: Biography

By: John T. Mason, Jr.

Q: I'm delighted that we're going to do this series on your very exciting period with the Navy, but before we begin the story, would you tell me a little bit about your own personal background, your educational background?

Capt. T.: I'd be delighted, Dr. Mason, but in the beginning I'd like to say how much I appreciate the opportunity that has been afforded to me by the Naval Institute and yourself to record the experiences that I had during the war. I have felt for a long time that my experiences should be preserved inasmuch as they are the day-to-day operating experiences of a live Seabee battalion as averse to the chronology of the Seabee battalions as a whole, a number of which have already been published.

Q: Yes, and having gone through some of those you loaned me, they are rather pictorial in nature and the text isn't that extensive, so I'm very glad, too.

First, give me the date of your birth and place of

Triest #1 - 2

your birth.

Capt. T.: I was born in New York City in 1905, of a long line of engineers. My grandfather was Charles R. MacDonald, a very prominent civil engineer who went to Rensselaer Polytechnic Institute. His career was climaxed as President of the American Bridge Company and was largely linked up with Colonel Roebling of the Roebling Wire Works. He and Colonel Roebling, for example, spun the cables on the Brooklyn Bridge, I think about 1883. At that time, my father had just come over from Germany and got an independent subcontract from the American Bridge Company to put the floor in the Brooklyn Bridge, and, through that relationship, met my mother.

Q: On both sides!

Capt. T.: Yes. There were engineers on both sides of the family. My father's family came from Stettin in Germany, having originated in Belgium as far back as we can go, and my maternal grandfather was Scotch-English.

Q: Where did your father get his engineering education?

Capt. T.: My father got his engineering at a university in Germany, the name of which I do not know. He came over to this country about 1880 and proceeded to have a very illustrious career in the construction business.

Q: In the metropolitan area?

Capt. T.: In the New York metropolitan area principally. His firm from 1900 to 1920 was called Snare and Triest. My father took care of all the work on the east coast, and Mr. Snare took care of their jobs in Cuba and in South America. It's a constant thrill to me whenever I return to New York, where I lived actually until 1950, to see the myriad numbers of construction projects that my grandfather and my father before me completed, such as the Brooklyn Bridge, several miles of the New York City Lexington Avenue subway, the approaches to the Hellgate Bridge, a great number of pier sheds along the Hudson and East Rivers, the Bayway Bridge from Bayway, New Jersey to Staten Island, many bridges for the New York H & H Railroad, many highway bridges, dry docks in the Brooklyn Navy Yard, the Catskill Aqueduct way back in 1910, several miles of the Independent Subway System and so on.

My father finally retired in 1936 and I formed my own company. At that time I did the first job on the Queens midtown tunnel, which was a ventilation shaft and subsequently a section of the Core wall for the Merriman Dam in Lackawack, New York.

Construction jobs just before the war became so large

Triest #1 - 4

in scope that only big combines could handle them and as I didn't fit into this picture, I went about some other programs for a short period. I joined the Civil Engineer Corps in November 1941.

Q: With such a family background as you had, it was inevitable that you, too, should be an engineer. Where did you go to school?

Capt. T.: I went to the Hill School in Pottstown, Pennsylvania, followed by Rensselaer Polytechnic Institute. As I said before, my grandfather was graduated from Rensselaer Polytechnic and, at that time, actually was the oldest living graduate, having graduated in 1857, followed by my uncle who graduated about 1880 or 1881.

Q: Were you the only son?

Capt. T.: No, I originally had two brothers.

Q: Are or were they also engineers?

Capt. T.: No. One of them actually was killed on his honeymoon so his career was cut very short, and the other went into the oil business and had a very successful career in oil exploration.

Triest #1 - 5

Q: Well, now, this is background to your service in the Navy. So, shall we begin with that?

Capt. T.: Yes. Sir.

Q: You made overtures to the Navy early in 1941?

Capt. T.: Actually, I went to see Admiral Moreell, Chief of the Bureau of Yards and Docks, whom I had known quite well because of my association - his association - with my father during the period from 1921 to 1929 when my father was building cantonments and dry docks in the Philadelphia Navy Yard. Admiral Moreell used to come down to Monmouth Beach, New Jersey and spent the night with us on his way to an inspection trip in Philadelphia, and I used to drive them over. So I knew the admiral quite well and when I decided that I would join the Civil Engineer Corps, I went to Washington to see him. Correction - I made my decision to join and went to the Third Naval District in New York in March 1941, to see Admiral Whitney. Then, when I finally decided to get into uniform in October, I went to Washington and saw Admiral Moreell.

I had rather an interesting experience at that time. The admiral was most cordial in his greeting to me and offered me a choice as to my post. He said, you can either go to Pearl Harbor or to Quonset Point. I thought for a moment and decided I'd go to Quonset Point. This was now the latter part of October 1941. On the way downstairs, I stopped in to see an old friend, Lieutenant Commander, now admiral, Lewis Strauss, who was then chief of staff to the head of the Bureau of Weapons. Lewis asked me what I was doing and I said I was in Washington to see about getting into uniform and he said, "Well, gee, how about joining me?" I said, "I'm afraid it's a little too late because I've just signed up with Admiral Moreell for the Civil Engineer Corps."

He said, "How many stripes are they going to give you?" and I said, "Two." He said, "Heck, I can give you two and a half. Let me see what I can do." So he dialed Admiral Moreell's number and when the admiral answered, he said, "Chief, I've got an old friend down here, Bill Triest, whom I've known for many years. I'd like to have him as my assistant. I can give him two and a half stripes, but he tells me he's already signed up with you. Will you let him go?" . . .

"Yes, Sir! I understand, Sir."

Q: He was pretty emphatic!

Capt. T.: Very emphatic - no dice. I thanked him very much and that was the end of that.

Triest #1 - 7

Q: It was solely because of your connection with Admiral Moreell that you thought of the Navy rather than the Army?

Capt. T.: No, I've always been very partial to the Navy, and while I wasn't very much of a seaman in those days, at least I had known enough of what the Navy was doing to appreciate that I wanted a Navy life rather than the tents of the Army.

Q: Especially quonset huts! Well, it wasn't at all certain that hostilities were going to break out that year, so you delayed?

Capt. T.: I had delayed from March until October because the war wasn't very imminent at that point, but in October it seemed to me that it was very imminent and that I'd better get aboard as quickly as possible.

Q: So you actually went in in October and went to Quonset Point?

Capt. T.: I went to Quonset Point and reported there on, I think, November 6th, 1941.

Q: Was there any indoctrination in Navy ways?

Capt. T.: No, there was no indoctrination at all, except that when I reported - retracing my steps a minute - having been to Washington and been assured of my assignment and simply awaiting orders at that moment, I proceeded to get into uniform. I went to my tailor in New York and ordered a naval uniform - in other words, the requisite number of blues, khakis and whites, a bridge coat and so on. When I reported to Captain Raymond V. Miller, CEC, USN, who was the officer in charge of construction, the captain looked at me and he said:

"Well, Triest, you don't belong to me."

I said, "Sir, you're Captain Miller and this is certainly Quonset Point."

He said, "Yes, but you don't belong to me."

I said, "Well, Sir, I'm thoroughly confused. Here are my orders. Can you explain?"

He said, "I tell you what I'll do. If you get into proper uniform and report to my quarters at five o'clock we'll forget all about it."

"By getting into proper uniform," I asked, "what do you mean, Sir?"

He said, "If you look at my sleeve, you'll see that I have crossed palms and you have a star. A star means a line officer and you're Civil Engineer Corps!" And that was the extent of my indoctrination! I didn't even know how to salute. I didn't know anything at all, except common ordinary politeness!

Then at his cocktail party I met his command. At that time they were in the midst of building Quonset Point, which was subsequently used as a naval air station and also as a training facility for the AVS officers - aviation volunteer specialists - the so-called million-dollar babies. As you may know, the navy scoured the country for a special breed of cats - business executives, lawyers, bankers of the highest type - stealing a march on the Army. They really got the cream of the country to enlist in the AVS branch. These men went to Quonset Point and, after six weeks' very intensive indoctrination, were assigned to fleet posts, generally speaking as aides to the commanding officers of various ships afloat and shore establishments, where theoretically their special experience could be put to the best use.

Q: Gus Reid was active in that program, was he not?

Capt. T.: Gus Reid?

Q: Yes, of Dillon Reid in New York.

Capt. T.: I don't remember his name particularly, but there was a great fellow named Jay Schefflein who was the commanding officer of the AVS school and later the Air Combat

Intelligence School. He did a magnificent job turning out a class every six weeks for a couple of years. I had the distinct privilege of lecturing to these classes, not as part of the staff but in a sort of advisory capacity. I lectured on advance base depot construction. In other words, what the Civil Engineer Corps role was to be in the war. Again, there was no indoctrination. It was simply a question of, "You're an engineer and you're a construction man, use your head and tell them what you think has to be done. No program has been written yet. Keep your notes."

Q: And you came to Quonset when there was nothing there?

Capt. T.: Quonset was being built at that time. I suppose it was about three-quarters built.

Q: A kind of prototype base, wasn't it?

Capt. T.: That's right, except that we didn't do any advance base work from there. Let me retrace my steps for a minute.

The first assignment I had when I went to Quonset was as budget officer. We had approximately a 70-million dollar budget for advance base depot design and construction including all necessary equipment and were administering a civilian contract underway by George A. Fuller and Merritt, Chapman & Scott. The huts in those days were first called Nissen Huts after the British huts and later became Quonsets. They came in many versions from living quarters to mess halls, kitchens, showers, hospital wards, operating rooms, morgues, et cetera. The equipment included landing mats, generator units, distillation units and construction equipment of all kinds - road graders, shovels, trucks, cranes, concrete mixers, welding equipment and so on and so on. Shortly after I got to Quonset, the construction of the Advance Base Depot, Davisville, was started, and the budget that had been assigned to Captain Miller, which by then had reached more than $400,000,000 (and in one year soared to $800,000,000) covered the initial phases of the development of living facilities, which were named, because of their location, quonset huts. The pontoons, without which we could not have won the war, were born here including the "Sea Horse" or giant outboard motor. This propulsion unit used to propel pontoon barges was the father of the present small boat outboard motor.

Q: I would presume that you were eminently qualified as a budget officer because you were accustomed to purchasing all sorts of construction materials?

Capt. T.: In a manner of speaking, "Yes," but "No," as I

had had no oil field experience, little maritime experience and no contact at all with personnel or troops in encampments. My heavy construction experience was, of course, a tremendous help, but I was thoroughly familiar with construction equipment of all kinds.

Within a month I was assigned as Domestic Project Manager for the work we were doing in Iceland, Ireland, and Scotland - these projects were known as F1-F2. The jobs entailed the design and construction of these bases by the civilian contractors that were building Quonset Point and Davisville - George A. Fuller and Merritt, Chapman and Scott, a joint venture.

Q: These advance bases in Iceland and other places were being built actually before we got into hostilities ourselves?

Capt. T.: There's no question about it. Actually, they were working in Iceland, Ireland, and Scotland under the contracts F1 and F2 to the best of my knowledge, ten months or a year before the war under so-called lend-lease.

Q: They were being built for the British, then?

Capt. T.: Well, ostensibly, yes, but actually we were shipping over Quonset Point equipment to many bases around the world by November 1941 - eventually as many as 120.

Q: Tell me about your involvement in those several projects.

Capt. T.: The first project I was assigned to, after my short term as budget officer, was the F1-F2 job and within a matter of a few days I learned that the progress on the job was completely unsatisfactory in that neither one of these contractors had ever been involved in the building of tank farms or pipelines, and this was a very serious deficiency which resulted in months and months of delay which nobody could afford at that time.

So I went to Captain Miller and reported that I thought the progress was entirely inadequate and from my examination of the plans the work was being designed by a stateside engineering force. They proposed to build the pipelines, for example, in Iceland as they would build them in the United States, in peace time using reinforced concrete duct work and so on. Then too, the designs were only about half-finished at that time and no construction had been started. The captain asked me what I proposed to do about it and I said, "the first thing I'll do is go out and get another contractor because, as I see the picture, we cannot go this slow and terribly expensive route. I think that we have to get a contractor that is thoroughly conversant with pipelines and tank farms and get on with the job."

He said, "What do you mean by that?" So I said, "Well, I would go to Standard Oil or Humble or Gulf or one of the oil companies that are in that business. I think they could give us the most help."

So, he said, "It's your baby. Go and see what you can do."

Q: Why had George A. Fuller, Merritt Chapman and Scott been chosen? Do you know?

Capt. T.: They were just a two large contractors banded together for financial and personnel reasons with wide expertise. Here were these enormous jobs to be let and even in November 1941 this job was a 70-million dollar contract.

Q: As I remember, George Fuller had been involved in all the new government buildings and that sort of thing. Merritt, Chapman was largely salvage, wasn't it?

Capt. T.: Merritt Chapman was a salvage company but actually had three or four divisions. One was the salvage division, which at that time was very big. Then they had an industrial building division and a heavy construction division. At least three that I know of - George A. Fuller was essentially a building contractor. The government, by force of necessity, had to find established contracters with established organizations to do these various jobs. There were a myriad number of jobs and most of them were involved in heavy construction. Pipelines and tank farms happened to be a new requirement, as far as the Navy was concerned.

Q: It occurs to me, why wouldn't an outfit like George Fuller enlist the services of adequate people for that kind of thing?

Capt. T.: NIH, not invented here, which we find every day throughout life. They felt that they were more than competent to do the job. That's all there is to it. The people who were in charge of their construction and their design divisions were people who were accustomed to building dams and roads and tunnels and bridges and so on, but not pipelines. The Navy had never had a use for a pipeline or a tank farm.

Q: Wasn't there a sense of urgency about these bases?

Capt. T.: Enormous urgency but, again, when you had an organization built up to their size - I think they had about 1,800 people in their offices and assembly plants at Quonset Point - it was natural to think that they could handle any assignment. Our work, however, was just too much of a divergency from their normal category of work.

Triest #1 - 16

Q: How did you go about involving Standard Oil under those circumstances? It must have been a touchy situation, wasn't it?

Capt. T.: It was an extremely touchy situation and I knew that I was treading on very thin ground, particularly wearing only two stripes. This was quite a plunge, but I said I'd do it, so I went to New York that night and to 1 Rockefeller Plaza the next day. Going to the principal information desk, I asked for the pipeline division. They sent me up to a man affectionately known as "Cap" Finney, who was in charge of pipelines and tank farms for Standard Oil Company of New Jersey. I told him my story in ten or fifteen minutes and said that I'd like him to consider helping us with the design of the tank farms and pipelines that were necessary for Iceland, Ireland and Scotland.

Q: In conjunction with the contractors who were already on the spot?

Capt. T.: No, their responsibility would be design only. I didn't want to put the construction burden on them. I said, "Will you take this on? George A. Fuller and Merritt, Chapman & Scott have the construction contract but the job is hopelessly hung up on the design and is now over six months behind. Principally because they're not experienced in this particular business, and I feel that you're eminently qualified - can do the job if you will." He said, "Okay, we will."

Then I said, "Next, I think we must discuss the question of fees. This is an unsolicited contract on your part and there's no possibility of bidding on it or coming up with a formal proposal. It'll have to be on a cost-plus basis because we don't know ourselves what we're getting into."

He said, "Okay, we'll do it on a cost-plus basis and for a fee of one dollar." So I said, "That suits us. I'll check with Captain Miller and I'll let you know tomorrow."

I went back and reported to Captain Miller and we had an hour's discussion on the subject. I convinced him that that was the way we should go. The next day we made a formal arrangement with Standard and canceled the original contractors design phase.

Q: Was that a difficult thing to achieve, to cancel out part of the original contract?

Capt. T.: No. I think that the original contractors had very little objection. They realized that they were in water over their depth. I wasn't in on that cancellation, but by that time the money was rolling in so fast and there was so much other work to do that I think they were glad to be relieved of it. Now, this was design only. This was not construction.

Q: They didn't actually have men on the ground?

Capt. T.: Oh, they had men up there in Iceland, oh, yes, but they were doing and they continued to do the construction not only of the tank farms designed by Standard but the airfield at Reykjavik port facilities, camps, et cetera. The contract that I gave Standard Oil was simply for the design. Then, when the plans were completed, they turned over their plans to the contractors in Quonset Point who proceeded to buy the materials and ship them to Iceland. This design work is what I was particularly concerned with other than getting the actual material shipped.

Q: How did you and the captain succeed in waiving the usual red tape in such things with Washington?

Capt. T.: I think the whole thing has to be credited to Admiral Moreell, a perfectly extraordinary individual and a man who had great, great strength and who commanded great respect from the entire naval organization. What he asked, no matter whether it was from Admiral King or the Bureau of Personnel or whomever, he got.

To continue with my story of F1-F2. I returned to New York the next day and was introduced to a chap named Charlie Adoue, who was assigned to this project by Cap Finney.

Q: He was a Standard Oil man?

Triest #1 - 19

Capt. T.: He was one of their leading designers. He had just returned from Aruba and was put in charge of this contract.

Q: May I ask, did you have any knowledge of pipelines and tank farms yourself?

Capt. T.: None whatsoever, but I recognized the knowledge that the Standard Oil people had and was willing to take their recommendations. They assigned Charlie Adoue to me and Cap Finney gave him carte blanche to do as he saw fit. The first thing he had to do was to accumulate a design force, so he and Cap Finney talked it over at length and very quickly began to bring in people from around the world that they could spare from other projects. Pretty soon they had about eighteen engineers and draftsmen and we had a section of the thirty-first floor of 1 Rockefeller Plaza assigned to us. In addition, Cap Finney assigned his personel secretary to me and we soon dubbed her "Admiral" - Admiral French.

At any rate, we got going with the F1-F2 program by working many long hours each day, and at the end of about a month were very well along with the drawings and had actually been feeding the information to the contractors for the purchase of equipment in the intervening period.

Q: May I ask, was there any work to be undone? These contractors had been involved in these projects for some time. Did you have to undo some of the things they had done?

Capt. T.: No, Sir. Actually this tank farm and pipelines had not been started. The airfield work however, and other projects were going well. In the oil field work we weren't going to build any reinforced concrete troughs to put pipe in with covers on and that sort of thing. We were simply going to bury the pipes in the ground. Instead of making nice neat layouts for the work, we left a lot of that up to the forces in the field - to take the shortest line between two points rather than to build by stateside standards.

Q: What I meant was, hadn't they already begun their construction?

Capt. T.: No, nothing in being, so we didn't waste any money in that respect.

Then comes a very interesting story. It's really the first project that was specifically my own. On Christmas Eve, I believe it was - no, it was on New Year's Eve 1941, I got a call from my counterpart in the Bureau of Yards and Docks in Washington, Lieutenant Commander Wayne van Leer, who was a deputy, I guess you'd call him, to Captain Everett Huntington, who was in charge of the advance base section of the Bureau of Yards and Docks. He asked for Captain Miller and unfortunately the captain was out on some inspection trip, so he said, "Well, I'll have to talk to you. Get some pencils and a sheaf of paper because we're going to be talking for some times."

Well, for four hours he dictated the requirements for a super secret base to be known as "Bobcat" which was to be built in the Christmas Islands one thousand miles south of Honolulu - as the first fueling station on the way to Australia.

Q: And it was so urgent that it had to be done over the telephone?

Capt. T.: It was that urgent. As a matter of fact, the timetable was that we were to design all the construction facilities, including the tank farm, pipelines, submarine-loading facilities - by "submarine" I mean submarine hoses out to buoys in the harbor for refueling ships - and the equipment necessary to build an airfield, hospital, living facilities for 5,000 Army personnel, and this all had to be done and the equipment accumulated - about 20,000 tons of it - and loaded on two ships in Quonset Point in two weeks - I repeat, in two weeks!

Q: It sounds like an impossible job. Were you not appalled at this?

Capt. T.: I was too green to be appalled! At any rate, the captain came back and I told him that I had had this long conversation with Commander van Leer and showed him my sheaf of notes and told him of the urgency of the job. At that point, the captain grew crimson and asked why van Leer didn't speak to him, and I said, "Well, Captain, he wanted to speak to you very badly but unfortunately you were on inspection and I couldn't reach you. The commander insisted on talking to me about it because he was going to have to give me the details anyway. He asked me to convey his regrets he couldn't talk to you directly, but the result is that here are the specifications, here is the urgency for it," and so on.

At that point the captain became, of course, very much interested in the project, as I had become, and said, "Well, go ahead. Do anything that's necessary."

Q: In retrospect, when was this plan born in Washington?

Capt. T.: This plan was probably born in Washington just about the 25th of December 1941, and the word to go ahead was given to me on the 31st.

Q: Did this mean that you ceased to be interested in Iceland, Ireland and Scotland?

Capt. T.: Not at all. It was my continuing baby, but by

Triest #1 - 23

that time we'd had a month of this thing. As I said, before, we were very well along with our designs and had been able to feed sufficient information to the contractors to keep them busy for some time. So it was felt that we could divert our efforts in favor of Bobcat particularly as it had such a special priority.

Q: How large a staff did you have at that point?

Capt. T.: I had two secretaries in Quonset Point plus the staff of eighteen that Charlie Adoue had been able to assemble in New York. The captain asked me what my plans were and I said, "Well, the only thing I think we can do is to go right to Standard Oil or one of the majors and have them undertake it." Of course, the same procedure would prevail. We would design in New York, turn the construction requirements over to the procurement staff of George A. Fuller and Merritt, Chapman and Scott, and they would then accumulate the material and load it aboard ships and ship it out.

I went to New York that afternoon and met Charlie Adoue about four o'clock.

Q: This would be on New Year's Day?

Capt. T.: This was on New Year's Day. I laid the whole program out to him and said that this was a Triple A priority program

Triest #1 - 24

as far as we were concerned (with only an A rating) and we had to stop what we were doing on F1-F2 in order to get this job out and we had just two weeks in which to do it.

Further, one of the specifications was that we were to recruit an engineer whom we could commission to build it because, in searching through their files, the Navy found they didn't have a single construction man who was in any way familiar with pipelines and tank farms - none. Also, they could find no welders who were to be an essential part of this job - you couldn't pry a welder loose from a shipyard to save your soul. There were precious few qualified construction men loose and the Navy had none other than in shipyards. So the second most important part of our job was to conscript the first construction detachment to send out in uniform, of course, to build these facilities. The contractors were not going to build.

Q: Were they called "Seabees" at that point?

Capt. T.: No. They were called a construction detachment, because it had been envisioned that construction battalions would be formed which would consist of five companies each. I don't know whether we called this a "detachment" or a "company" at that time, but these were construction people, actual mechanics, under Civil Engineering Corp Officers, versus CEC officers who were supervisory personnel in the United

States in the shipyards and Public Works offices and so on. Admiral Moreell actually started using Naval Construction personnel at the end of World War I.

Anyway we worked, all of us, most of that night to get the basic layout and essential plans committed to paper. We'd been told by the Bureau that the only map or drawing of the island was an old German geographical study which had been made some twenty or thirty years before, and there were no pictures available except a motion picture called "Tabu." "Tabu" was just a Hollywood film made on the island -

Q: It actually had been made on the island?

Capt. T.: It had been made on the island five or six years before. We viewed the movie, of course, and it gave us an idea of the terrain. This was a great help as there were no topographical maps available.

Q: ONI didn't have anything?

Capt. T.: Nothing, absolutely nothing. ONI was just a small arm or branch of the service at that time. We had to guess at the height of the hills on the island so as to get some perspective to determine how we could sink the fuel tanks into the side of the hills for camouflage purposes - a specific requirement - and the distance from the hills to the waterfront.

Then we had to estimate the distance out to the ships to judge the lengths of hose lines for fueling purposes. This was all conjecture. We had nothing to go on.

Q: Who owned Christmas Island? Who claimed Christmas Island?

Capt. T.: I don't know.

Q: The U.S.?

Capt. T.: I think probably we did. I don't think there was any international complication about our going in. All we found there were a few dozen natives.

In any event we set about getting the design force working on this thing as soon as we'd viewed the motion picture. Then Charlie and I turned our attention to recruiting personnel, including the principal officers necessary to build this base. We had to have what is called a "pipeline superintendent".

Q: How many men did you anticipate?

Capt. T.: To do what?

Q: To do the job.

Capt. T.: Oh, well, we planned to send out a detachment or

company of about 250 men with the requisite number of officers, but the principal officer had to be a tank farm man. We talked this over with Cap Finney and he said, "Well, there's one man we have named "shorty" Duddleston who is our superintendent on the Portland-Montreal pipeline and he's about finished up there. (That was a 20-inch pipeline they were just completing between Portland, Maine, and Montreal.) I suggest you call him up and see what you can do."

So I got on the telephone and told him what was happening - that the Navy had a very special job that I was assigned to, and one of our assignments was the recruiting of an officer with pipeline and tank farm experience to get into uniform and go out with a uniformed force to build these facilities. He said, "You couldn't pay me enough to do that. I'm getting $25,000 a year. What would you pay me?" I said, "I really don't know. $6,000 or $7,000. But you have to consider the urgency of the mission and the needs of your country. I'll talk to Standard Oil about it and they'll do something for you but I don't know what, but I can't offer you any more than your rank would command." He said, "What kind of rank are you offering me?" I thought quickly and tongue in cheek said, "Two and a half stripes," knowing full well that the Navy wasn't giving any more than two stripes to officers being recruited at that time.

Anyway, he said, "I'll think it over. Call me back." So we arranged to call him back in the morning when we had another twenty-minute conversation and by the time I'd finished he had agreed to take on the job. He said, "All right, I'll be in New York Sunday morning," which was the next day. So on Sunday morning he came into the office about eight o'clock and we worked all day and laid the whole thing out for him, even though he was a civilian and this was a top secret job. We hadn't time to get him a clearance, in addition he told me that he wasn't physically fit and would probably need a lot of medical waivers and so on. When it got down to cases I found out that he had no more than a high-school education, and this was another road block.

Q: Indeed it was!

Capt. T.: Because no officer was given a commission unless he had a college degree or the equivalent thereof. Anyway, the long and short of it was that we worked all day and he was thoroughly indoctrinated as to what had to be done and how fast.

Then he asked the sixty-four dollar question, "Where are you going to get the men?" and I said, "We're going to get the men out of the receiving barracks in Charleston and we're going to recruit welders. We know we've got to get a welding chief for you and as many other welders as we can and I propose to go to the oilfields in Louisiana and Texas and get them that way."

Triest #1 - 29

Q: Take them from industry?

Capt. T.: Yes, because as I said there were none available in this part of the country at all on account of the shipbuilding business.

Q: I take it from this that the normal operations of Standard Oil and others came almost to a halt?

Capt. T.: No, because these men were drawn one at a time from numerous operations around the world, so it really didn't affect them. In other words, nobody is indispensable and if they drew one man out of an eight man office and another man out of six, and another man out of four, it really wasn't very much of a wrench as far as they were concerned. Charlie Adoue had just completed a job and so had Duddleston, so that those two men had not been reassigned.

Anyway, we took a sleeper to Washington. By pre-arrangement we were to meet Admiral Moreell and Captain Huntington on Monday morning at eight o'clock. We arrived about five minutes of eight and van Leer was jumping up and down in the Bureau of Yards and Docks and so was Captain Huntington, and they said, "For God's sake, the Admiral and Admiral King are waiting for you upstairs. The chief's room number if 4645." At the same time, I had brought "Admiral" French, my secretary, down because every spare moment I was dictating memorandums to her and the idea was that she could transcribe them when we were there, and be available to take more dictation. I was in the meantime covering all this with orders to the contractors. So I said, "If you'll give 'Admiral' French a desk and a typewriter she can go to work while we're busy." Okay, so that was that.

I went up with Duddleston to see the admiral. Duddleston was still in civilian clothes, of course. We went into Admiral Moreell's office and his chief of staff, a commander, jumped up and said, "Oh, my goodness, yes, the admiral's waiting for you." He knocked on the door and Admiral Moreell opened the door himself and right behind him was another very distinguished admiral whom I learned was Admiral King. We walked in and I introduced them to Duddleston and Admiral King said, "Come in Son, come in. Just the man we're waiting for." And as I stood there, Admiral King put his arm round one shoulder and Admiral Moreell put his around the other shoulder and the three of them walked to the window - to the admiral's desk - where they all sat down. I stood there first on one foot and then the other while they talked to him, and they began describing the job immediately.

As he sat there, with his hat in his hand, Duddleston said, "Well, gentlemen, I'm still a civilian. I'm not cleared for this sort of thing." The admiral said, "Pay no attention to that. We'll take care of it. Triest, you can be excused now. We'll talk." So I went down to the Bureau of Yards and

Docks and for about three hours talked and dictated some more and discussed the job with van Leer and Captain Huntington. Then they called me back upstairs about twelve or one o'clock and Admiral Moreell said, "Triest, Duddleston is going to join us and I want you to get him in uniform by five o'clock this afternoon." "Yes, Sir."

So I took him down to see Commander Perry who was our liaison between the Bureau of Yards and Docks and the Bureau of Personnel. Commander Perry said, "What's this all about?" and I said, "I've got a man here that I've got to get in uniform. He is going out to Bobcat, and it's extremely urgent, as you may have heard, and I have to have him in uniform by five o'clock."

"What!" he said, "that's impossible. You know the procedure around here."

I said, "I'm sorry, Sir, but if you'll just call Admiral Moreell he'll tell you himself." So he dialed and said, "Chief, Lieutenant Triest is down here with a man he wants - yes, Sir, yes, Sir." And that was that!

He started filling out the necessary forms, name, address, education? "High school." "You know this is impossible. I can't get a commission for a man who hasn't had a college education."

I said again, "I'm sorry, but you heard the admiral."

"Yes, I heard him."

He filled out the form a little further and then said,

"Now how about the letters of recommendation? I've got to have five letters of recommendation." I said, "Well, Admiral King will give him one, Admiral Moreell another, Captain Huntington and Commander van Leer and I'll give him one." More disgusted grunts and then, Okay, okay. How about a physical?" I said, "Well, Sir, he hasn't had a physical, obviously." He said, Well, take him down to see Captain So-and-So in charge of the infirmary on the first floor." I went to the infirmary and spoke to the Chief who was the captain's chief yeoman, and said, "I'd like to speak to the captain," and he said, "I'll take care of it." I said, "Maybe I'd better speak to the captain because this is a rather unusual and urgent matter. I have to have this man in uniform - a complete physical and in uniform in about two and a half hours. I just think I'd better talk to the captain."

So I was ushered into the captain's office, and here was a big, florid-faced gentleman. I told him my problem and he said, "This is highly unusual." I said, "I appreciate that, Sir, but it has to be done." So he said, "Well, how about his physical qualifications?" and Duddleston said:

"Captain, let me interrupt. I'm color blind, I'm flat-footed, I'm knock-kneed, I have less than half my teeth, and whatever else may be wrong, I don't know, but I'm in fine shape."

He said, "This is impossible. You know that," and I

said, "Yes, Sir, I know. Would you mind calling Admiral Moreell and he will straighten it out." So he called Admiral Moreell and he said, "Chief, Lieutenant Triest - " and the same rigmarole - "Yes, Sir, yes, Sir, right away."

So he called his staff in and gave them instructions to give Duddleston a physical and make it as complete as they could within an hour's time. He successfully passed with eight waivers.

At four o'clock, then, having reported back to the Bureau of Yards and Docks, the thing was underway and I went back to New York to get on with my work and Duddleston was to call me at seven-thirty. In the meantime I had called my tailor in New York and gave him the story and ended with his promise to keep three men overtime to fit the uniforms. Duddleston was to call me with his measurements by five o'clock and was due back in New York by 10.

Q: By ten the next morning?

Capt. T.: No, ten that night. From five thirty then until ten we had to get him in uniform and ready to go.

He called on schedule and he had two secretaries in the Bureau of Yards and Docks taking his measurements according to the tailor's instructions over the telephone - the height, chest, waist and there was a bit of a do when the tailor asked for the inside leg measurement and so on - and I relayed these to the tailor.

Q: Did you have any great problem in recruiting the necessary welders and so forth for the project?

Capt. T.: Just let me give you one little story.

When Duddleston arrived in New York at ten-thirty that night, "Admiral" French and I went with him to the tailor's where literally he was fitted to his clothes. They were completed except for one or two small things, but by eleven o'clock he was ready to go with three or four packages which we helped him carry. There he was in uniform with his cap on at a jaunty angle –

Q: Did he know how to salute?

Capt. T.: He'd had no indoctrination whatsoever. We got down on the sidewalk and he said, "Say, you know, I don't even know how to salute. What do I do when they salute me?"

I said, "You just follow them. Here's a man coming right now. There's a gob across the street, standing there with his hands in his pea jacket. You start across the street when he does and you just watch him, and when he salutes you, you answer. Don't salute first. Wait till he salutes you and you answer."

We stood there with great amusement watching Duddleston itching to go, waiting for the light on 52nd Street and Madison Avenue, and as the light changed the gob started to cross the street and Duddleston, too. We could see Duddleston's right hand getting ready to salute all the way across the street. In the meantime, the gob had his hands still in his jacket and his white hat cocked at an angle, and a big plug of tobacco in his mouth. As he walked across the street, his eye caught Duddleston, and he turned his head the other way and let out a big plop of tobacco juice, didn't bother to salute, or raise his hand or anything, but Duddleston was so anxious that he saluted anyway! We just stood there and roared, absolutely roared. I was in uniform, too, you see! It was a terribly funny incident.

Q: Once he was equipped with uniforms, where did he go?

Capt. T.: He boarded a special plane we had chartered and went to Fort Worth to say goodbye to his family. The plane waited and the next morning took him to Charleston. I went back to the office in New York and the next day to Quonset. In fact, I was back and forth to Quonset almost every day during that period. I remember I kept a couple of secretaries busy about ten hours a day doing the most horrendous job. They had to make twenty-eight copies of every memorandum and every order issued. Twenty-eight copies!

Q: Without benefit of Xerox!

Capt. T.: Without benefit of any duplication equipment - to be supplied to the various departments of the contractors' organization, not only for purchasing, but for engineering review, expediting, and so on and so on.

Q: This was peacetime practice that continued on?

Capt. T.: Right. No, I wouldn't say that. I'd say that seven tenths of it was born of wartime requirements, because the expediters had to have copies of all purchase orders, and the shippers had to have copies - all this stuff was specially handled - and the transportation people, eight or ten copies went to the transportation people by themselves.

Anyway, within a few days, we had developed the specifications for the various pieces of equipment required, starting with the longest lead-time items such as National Transit pumps necessary for pumping the fuel oil through the submarine loading hose to the tanks on shore.

Q: Whose wisdom was able to establish that kind of priority?

Capt. T.: It was Charlie Adoue's business and I took his lead completely. He knew exactly what had to be done. In a matter of a few hours he had the whole thing laid out in his mind as to what was necessary. So he issued the basic orders I gave to the contractors. In the meantime, they had to find sources of supply. In many cases, however, we supplied the sources because they were not familiar with either the tank farm business or the pipeline business. National Transit Pumps, to them, were Greek words.

Anyway, the contractors had fifty expediters busy expediting my orders to the various manufacturers and suppliers throughout the country, including, for example, the purchase and transportation of steel tanks which we had to buy in Texas and have trucked to Quonset. The submarine loading hose we got from Hewitt-Robbins in Buffalo, and they had to have special priorities. Actually, we only had a 1A priority, that's all we could get. They were making hose for the Air Force with a 3A priority, so I had to spend literally hundreds of dollars telephoning to the resident naval inspectors of these various plants to persuade them that ours was a really much more urgent program than any that they were working on.

Q: How did you bridge the gap of secrecy in such instances?

Capt. T.: I simply said that I was working on the highest priority job that the Civil Engineer Corps had under direct orders from Admiral Moreell and Admiral King, and they just had to get it out, and in one week including trucking to Quonset.

Q: Why didn't Yards and Docks help you in that by giving

you a higher priority?

Capt. T.: They couldn't get it. In other words, the highest priorities were going to naval aviation supplies and army aviation supplies. The 3-A priority was tantamount to the most urgent requirements the country had. It was just laid at my door to persuade the naval inspectors that ours was equally important and somehow had to be worked in. I called the resident inspector at the National Transit Company about the pumps and he said, "Well, we have to have bearings. We have no bearings for these pumps." Where do the bearings come from? Well, the bearings were coming from Hyatt Roller Bearing. So I called the Hyatt Roller Bearing Company and spoke to the resident inspector there, and he said, "We're backed up with triple-A priority bearings for the next four months. We couldn't think of giving them to you." I said, "Come on, now, get down to earth. We have to have them and I don't want to have to go to the White House to get orders directly to you to get those bearings. We have to have the pumps and, if necessary, I'll go through Admiral King to the White House. This is my job and it's going to be done. We have to have those bearings, and they must be delivered to National Transit in three days."

And so it went with everything that we asked for. The long and short of it was that within ten days something around 18,000 tons of equipment had been accumulated, either

Triest #1 - 39

by direct purchase on the outside or by taking it from stock at Quonset Point, Davisville. And the ships were there, two freighters. We loaded about 9,000 tons on each freighter.

Let me go back one step.

In the meantime, having recruited Duddleston, then it became necessary to find a welder, a chief welder that we could also get into uniform, and I think I spent some $1,500 in seven days on the telephone calling up every construction company and every oil company that I could find in the registers, all over, from La Grange, Georgia, to Tulsa, Oklahoma, to Gulfport, to New Orleans, et cetera.

Q: Standard couldn't help you there?

Capt. T.: They couldn't help me in that respect at all so I had to help myself. I'd get a lead on a man and they'd say, well, he's out in the field and I can't reach him but he lives in such and such a place and he generally has dinner at such and such a tavern, or something, and he's generally there around six o'clock. So I would call that tavern at six o'clock and get him on the phone. I talked to about twenty of them but I couldn't persuade them to save me. Finally, I found a man that I did persuade to join up. He asked me what he should do and so on, and I said, "Say goodbye to your family. We'll pay your fare, of course, to Charleston, South Carolina, and you report there in two days and start your school." This was a real breakthrough and with his help I finally got a half dozen more with the inevitable hassle about medical waivers.

In the meantime we had conscripted 250 men from various receiving stations in New York and Charleston and other places, and they were all shipped to Charleston. Then three or four other officers were assigned to Duddleston from the Civil Engineer Corps. I never knew their names. They started in Charleston getting these forces into some shape, seeing to their equipment and so on.

Then we loaded all kinds of steel plate and angles on board so additional men could be taught welding. They figured that they had to have about seventeen welders and the chief's responsibility was to train these man (drafters) en route. So we had welding equipment, including generators and so on, on deck, and they set up schools on one of the two ships to train the boys in the art of welding between Charleston, South Carolina, and Bora Bora.

Q: This was a matter of weeks —

Capt. T.: This was a matter of about two and a half to three weeks, going through the Canal and on out there.

Q: Was there a special escort for these two merchant ships,

because this was going through submarine-infested waters, wasn't it?

Capt. T.: No, not in those days. This was in a line between the Panama Canal and Bora Bora and that was relatively free from submarines.

Q: But I mean from Charleston down?

Capt. T.: No, the Germans had not penetrated this far, at least at that time.

Now, to go back again, there's a cargo story which is rather an interesting one!

We, as I say, accumulated about 18,000 tons of equipment and stowed it aboard these two vessels at Quonset Point and they sailed on time, but there were still 2,000 tons that couldn't make it. It was being trucked in from various places around the country. There was no doubt that we had to get this equipment aboard those vessels and so we accumulated a convoy of 400 trucks with two drivers each, 110 gallons of gasoline in drums, box lunches, and water and loaded all this material on the 400 trucks. We started them off in convoy and they went directly from Quonset Point, right through New York City, on down to Charleston, South Carolina, in two and a half days, stopping only twice, I think for more fuel. They took turns sleeping and they were met at every state line by state troopers. They went through New York City as one solid convoy, 400 trucks, across the George Washington Bridge! Anyway, they got there on time, they put it on board in time, the men were there, and we got back only one telegram saying that one valve, or some small part, was missing. That was the only feedback that we had.

Q: Where was the ready cash obtainable for financing something like this?

Capt. T.: Through the contractors. In other words, they had this basic contract which, at that time, had grown from $700 million to some astronomical sum, but there was plenty of cash available.

That's what the contractors did, and they did a magnificent job in that respect. They could handle that. They knew that business - expediting materials, handling it, transportation and so on. That was their particular forte.

Q: There were no snags in the recruiting itself, in getting the necessary men?

Capt. T.: After I got the lead man?

Q: You said you had some difficulty in phoning all these welders all over the country. Did you stress patriotism to attract them?

Capt. T.: Oh, I had to do that to a very large extent.

Q: How effective was it as a note?

Capt. T.: Well, it was sufficiently effective to get Duddleston and this leading petty officer. Now, with the other people I really had problems. They either had sick families or were sole support or they were really in too bad shape themselves to get the necessary waivers, et cetera. There were extenuating circumstances all the way along. But when I got to the right men, I think the loyalty thing was the clincher.

Q: That was quite a project. What did it do to you personally? I mean, being under this tension all the time?

Capt. T.: I think I had about three or four hours sleep a night for those two weeks, but being young, strong, and full of adrenilin, I survived.

Q: You had a family of your own, did you not?

Capt. T.: No, I was a bachelor at that time.

Q: That was fortunate!

Triest #1 - 44

Capt. T.: Very fortunate, yes.

Q: Well, having seen these merchant ships loaded and on their way, what else did you have to do in connection with that particular project?

Capt. T.: When the ships were loaded at Charleston and left, that was it. Every piece of equipment that was left behind when the ships departed from Quonset was shipped overland by truck and it all arrived. We had no strings untied.

Q: What about the base itself? I mean, was it accomplished?

Capt. T.: The base was built. Duddleston did an excellent job. As a matter of fact, he went on from there to build eight or ten other fueling stations across the Pacific. I didn't see him again actually. I heard from him from time to time, but I didn't see him. I think he finished up Bora Bora about August of that year and was assigned to another base, and so on. And in November of 1942 I was myself assigned to a construction battalion - at that time they were called Seabees - so I got out of the design business and into the actual construction myself.

Q: But before you got out of the design business, there was

Triest #1 - 45

something else that came up, was there not?

Capt. T.: That's right. We finished F1-F2 - Iceland, Ireland, and Scotland.

Q: Did you travel to those places yourself?

Capt. T.: No. Fortunately, I had been to Iceland. I had gone there in 1929 so I had a very vivid picture of the terrain and the requirements, the soil there, the coastal conditions and so on. This stood me in very good stead. For example, Admiral Kuaffman - Admiral Reggie Kauffman - was the commanding officer of the naval base there. (Much later his son, Admiral Draper Kauffman was superintendent of the Naval Academy. He married my sister-in-law, Peggy Tuckerman, my wife's younger sister.) But in those days, of course, I didn't know the admiral and all I kept getting were requirements from the admiral by two or three-page cables with the things that he wanted for his base and, it being my job, I was required to supply them.

One of the things that the contractors wanted was a ship-to-shore telephone, and so it was decided that we would get a 25 watt sending station for shore use and three watt transmitters for the tugboats that were going back and forth between Reykjavik and Keflavik. The next job that came along was -

Triest #1 - 46

Q: The Ascension Island job. Tell me about that.

Capt. T.: Ascension Island, yes. We had a job to do there similar to Bora Bora but there wasn't the speed required. Again we had to accumulate all the equipment necessary to build the airfield, the Army installations, hospital, tank farm, pipelines, and loading facilities.

Q: That was a british Island. Did they have any installations there at all?

Capt. T.: There were none there when we started. As a matter of fact, I got a great thrill out of this job because later my brother became an ATC pilot and ferried 35 single-engined fighter planes across the Atlantic to England and Scotland and landed each time at Ascension.

Q: Were there any problems involved in that, being a lonely spot of land in the middle of the South Atlantic?

Capt. T.: No, as far as I know there were not. Actually, I left Quonset Point in the middle of this job and the design work was turned over to somebody else, with Standard Oil still doing their part.

Q: The construction work was a Navy job?

Triest #1 - 47

Capt. T.: A Navy job. Again, I don't know the details of it because I was shipped out by that time.

Q: You'd acquired a rather vast amount of operating experience Navy-wise in this brief year, hadn't you?

Capt. T.: In a short while! My military indoctrination didn't come until I got detached from Davisville and went to Norfolk to NCTC, where all the Civil Engineer Corps officers reported for training prior to assignment to battalions. I went there for three weeks, I believe, while we went through a basic indoctrination period. I'd been in for a year at that point, but the other boys were fresh-caught. They reported there and we went through the regular drill.

Q: That was a kind of a postgraduate course for you!

Capt. T.: Yes. Then each compliment of officers was assigned to a battalion by number and we reported back to NCTC Davisville, which was the construction camp for Seabees on the east coast. I was assigned as executive officer of the 57th Construction Battalion under Lieutenant Commander Dwight Hardman.

Q: This was the direction you wanted to go?

Capt. T.: Yes. I was afraid the war was going to pass me

Triest #1 - 48

by and I wanted to get into the action.

Triest #2 - 49

Interview #2 with Captain Willard G. Triest, CEC, USNR

Place: His office in Annapolis, Maryland

Date: Thursday morning, 20 July 1972

Subject: Biography

By: John T. Mason, Jr.

Q: Captain, it's good to see you this morning and to resume your most interesting story. Last time, you told me some of the preliminaries and when we broke off you were in Davisville, Rhode Island, getting ready for service in the Pacific. Do you want to resume at that point, Sir?

Capt. T.: All right, thank you. I've really forgotten how far I progressed in my experiences at Davisville, but I think that the last I spoke about was my experiences on the F1-F2 pipeline jobs and Bora Bora.

Q: Yes, you described those activities and the Ascension Island affair. You covered all of that and you were turning toward the Pacific.

Capt. T.: Okay. Actually, there's one more episode at Davisville I want to include, which was a mock enemy attack on the base.

Among my other duties at Davisville, they named me security officer and gave me a station wagon with a red light and a siren and so on. I had the fire department and the other security forces under my command, and it became apparent very quickly, as I had suspected, that the security there was practically zero. It was all well and good to have a chain-link fence around our 1,500 acres and have 150 Marines as a security guard for Davisville and adjacent Quonset Point, but unless any force is geared to up really protect the territory that they're supposed to protect through the leadership of somebody who's had that experience, it's difficult for them to appreciate just how dangerous the enemy can be.

So, within a few days I went to my commanding officer and told him that while I didn't know much about security, I knew enough to know that it would be the simplest thing in the world for anybody to gain access to the property, and if they once gained access there'd be nothing in the world to stop them from proceeding at will, because everybody was considered as one big, happy family. Once anybody was inside the gate, nobody was ever questioned as to their identity and they never had to wear badges or in any other way be scrutinized or identified - anybody could of course buy a uniform.

Q: There had been a number of instances of sabotage, had there not?

Capt. T.: There were reported instances of sabotage and/or

thievery, but there was nothing very tangible about it. It was taken very lightly, and the sabotage, if it were sabotage, was of small moment. Anyway he said, "What do you propose to do?" I said, "I would like to take fifty Seabees out of our training camp at NCTC and then alert everybody on the base that there's going to be an enemy attack. I'll direct the offensive and leave the defense to NCTC and the Marines. Let's see what happens."

He said, "All right," so I laid out a program together with two of my assistants, and decided that we'd have fifty Seabees dressed in coveralls that would be the saboteurs under the direction of two officers. The Marines with a number of Seabees and their officers were to guard. I'm trying to think of the words - there was one headquarters and three or four sectional shelters which had been built in anticipation of air raids or enemy attack, as part of an over-all plan. But the manning of those stations and what was going to happen if there was an attack had never been delineated.

In any event, we proceeded to set up this attack for seven o'clock one night, after the civilian force of 15,000 that were employed there had left the base, so as not to involve the civilians any more than possible. As our plans developed, I realized it was going to be quite a show, so I asked permission to invite the security officers from the First and Third Naval Districts which included Boston, Newport, New York, and they accepted. These were all captains and one or two of their staffs. We invited them to come at six o'clock one evening and gave them a very nice dinner in our cafeteria, and I announced that at seven o'clock the raid would start and that I had assigned I think it was three command cars to take them wherever they wanted to go. The cars were manned by Seabees with white brassards on their sleeves indicating that they were judges and there were a number of other Seabees that were assigned to various posts around the base all equally established with white brassards, and then I left.

I knew vaguely what the plan of the attackers would be. They would attack by sea, and a defending force of five hundred Seabees were assigned to this particular duty plus 150 Marines who were scattered around strategically.

Well, the sabateurs did a very clever job. Five or six of them came ashore in a small boat - this was a dark night - and one of the patrol cars going along the beach road spotted them and the three men manning the command car got out and rushed to the water's edge and captured the so-called advancing enemy. The judge or monitor that was with the invading party pronounced them captured and they were therefore out of action. In the meantime, three other boats containing the other 47 saboteurs landed down the beach 100 and 200 yards and within a few minutes they had captured the command car and away they went.

Q: The first contingent acted as a decoy?

Capt. T.: Exactly. So the other fellows scattered around the place and carrying their sabotage equipment. Within a few minutes - I happened to be near the command headquarters at that time - dynamite charges started going off, felling trees across the roads. And incidentally, those dynamite charges - they used I think about five hundred pounds of dynamite in various places - rattled the countryside to such a degree that window panes even in Newport were rattled. Of course, the switchboards were crowded with calls, everybody thinking that the Martians had landed, for sure.

The saboteurs focused their attention immediately on the fire houses. We had I think two or three fire houses and they were captured immediately. That meant that the fire engines were out of commission. Another group set fire to an old barn more or less in the center of the area and that fire raged unattended. In the meantime in the command headquarters calls began coming in frantically from the various substations around. At the same time, when everybody's attention was focused on the telephone calls, the saboteurs snuck up behind the Marines guarding the headquarters and captured them.

Capt. T.: Captured all the guards. The Marine colonel and his staff were all inside feverishly answering telephone calls and paying no attention to what went on outside. So two Seabees marched into the headquarters and captured the whole bloody business, including the colonel. They were still permitted to answer the telephone as though nothing had transpired.

In the meantime word got around that the inspection party - the security officers hadn't been seen for some half-hour or so - and at that point I decided I'd better find out where they were. I couldn't go up and down the roads any more because the roads were all blocked by the felled trees. So I got on the telephone and found out that - from one substation - yes, a party of the enemy had appeared at the substation and they'd been locked up. I said, "Were these gentlemen in uniform?" and they said yes. So I went to this particular substation and was met by the lieutenant, who gave me a snappy salute, and I said, "Lieutenant, have you got somebody locked up around here?" "Yes, Sir, we have." I said, "Who is it?" He replied, "Well, there are about four captains and some commanders." I said, "You've got them locked up?"

He said, "Yes, Sir, they're in the the ammunition depot over there."

"What were the circumstances?"

"I think I'd better open the door and let you get the story firsthand."

So he opened the door and the "enemy" came out. The principal security officer was a captain from the First Naval District. He was so mad, I've never seen anybody so mad in my life - just fit to be tied. I said, "Captain there must be some mistake."

And the lieutenant said, "Sir, these gentlemen presented

themselves to me and I asked for their identification cards and found that they were not properly identified and so by the rules of the raid they were imprisoned."

I said, "What do you mean, they weren't properly identified?" I think the captain exploded at that point, and the lieutenant said, "Captain, we had an ALNAV last week saying that hereafter all identification cards had to have two grommets. Your identification cards are still of the old type and they only have one grommet."

The captain said, "Lieutenant, I commend you. Your boys have done a fine job. No hard feelings."

This was one of the great moments, you know. The chap had done his job and received praise.

Anyway, at that point, a review of that whole episode the next day made it abundantly clear that the security not only at our station but every station along the coast was woefully lacking.

Q: It was shockingly clear!

Capt. T.: It was shockingly clear. They even captured two Marines who were manning the main gate. There wasn't anybody left free. In other words, the whole place could easily have been destroyed.

Q: I suppose that situation had developed because the enemy

was far away?

Capt. T.: Yes, they'd hardly heard of the enemy. We're a peace-loving people and we trust everybody. Anyway, vastly improved security measures were installed there as well as in a great many other places under the cognizance of these particular officers. I don't know the details, but I've heard since that this made a lasting impression on a lot of people.

Q: It certainly should. I would think, however, that it would be difficult over a long period of time to maintain a level of security?

Capt. T.: It obviously was, and it would be even today. It's just impossible. We're not geared that way as a people. I mean, the German SS forces and the Russians have been trained that way from babyhood and are constantly being drilled in it, and, of course, it becomes second nature to them, but we're just not built that way. Many, many times as we went forward in the war in the Pacific I observed the same thing. Almost nonexistent security.

Q: But I imagine it tightened the closer you got to the actual enemy?

Capt. T.: That's right.

Q: Well, that was an astounding success!

Capt. T.: Then we embarked for Gulfport and continued our so-called training there by having our people operate equipment and build roads and do common construction problems aiding and abetting the construction of the base. This was a little difficult because the civilian contractors muzzled everything, so to speak. They fought the armed forces' doing any work, any construction work. This was one of the crosses that we had to bear throughout because the unions were so strong that they were just dictating.

Q: And they wouldn't relax in time of war?

Capt. T.: We forced them to finally, we maneuvered them into a position where they were able to do it without losing face, but it was a difficult problem. So we didn't get nearly the training that we should have gotten. The only thing they didn't interfere with was when we were doing pipe work or welding or things like that, which was not part of the construction contract of the base.

Q: You did engage in some specialized training of certain of the men for particular jobs?

Capt. T.: Yes. We had, of course, determined that we were

going to have a number of tractors, bulldozers and scrapers and so on, and we had to train a great many people in use of this equipment. We had a lot of trained bulldozer operators and crane operators and so on, but not nearly enough, and so we had to take so-called apprentices, fellows that had been apprentices in civilian life or just mechanics and try to speed up their education to make trained operators out of them.

Q: There was a decided attempt, then, to find men with the proper aptitudes?

Capt. T.: In the very beginning we had lengthy interviews with the boys and put them, from the very beginning, into categories that we knew they were best fitted for. This was one of the tremendous things that Admiral Moreell instituted when he first started. I don't know whether I've referred to this before or not, but Admiral Moreell agreed with the Bureau of Personnel that each Seabee commander would be privileged to re-classify any of his personnel to any grade that he saw fit the first time. Thereafter, they would have to advance in the prescribed manner. What I mean by that is this - we could take a 2nd Class seaman and make him a chief petty officer in his first re-grading.

Q: An arbitrary act?

Capt. T.: An arbitrary act approved by the Bureau of Personnel. We'll say we had jumped a man from 2nd Class seaman to 2nd Class petty officer, well, then, he could be jumped to 1st Class petty officer and then to chief petty officer only in proper sequence. But the first re-grading was very important. I don't know whether by official edict or whether we decided it, but it was decided there would be no re-grading the wrong way - I can't think of the word at the moment. What do we call it?

Q: Downgrading?

Capt. T.: No, it isn't downgrading. There's a special word. We decided we would do nothing for the first six weeks and in that six weeks' period, we not only observed the men in action on mock construction jobs and/or real, whenever - we were able to at Gulfport - but when we got overseas, observing these fellows in actual operation and therefore when we made the first reclassification. "Reclassification" it's called. When we made the first reclassification, then we did it according to the combined judgment of company officers and so on. As a matter of fact, in our particular case, I think we took about fifteen 2nd Class seamen and jumped them to chief petty officers, and another large group of 1st and 2nd Class seamen to 1st Class petty officers, and so on. So there was a great reshuffling the first time, which was a great morale

Triest #2 - 60

booster, because by that time the other fellows knew who knew what, and when you said that a man who'd only been a 2nd Class seaman should become a chief petty officer, he'd more or less established himself as a man of authority and experience with his peers. So, from the morale point of view, there was no grumbling at all that I knew of because we spent a lot of time on this and everybody was put in his proper slot. We tried to put square pegs in square holes and round pegs in round holes, that's what it amounted to.

Q: And those who didn't make it at that point could say, it might happen to me, too."

Capt. T.: That's correct. It was a very successful way to operate. Very successful, and that set the tone of the whole corps, really. We departed for overseas at that point.

Q: How long were you in Gulfport?

Capt. T.: I think we were in Gulfport three or four weeks.

Q: That was quite a transition from winter in Rhode Island, wasn't it?

Capt. T.: It was, indeed, but I don't think anybody really paid much attention to that. We were too busy with our work

Triest #2 - 61

and organization and so on. Then we went to San Francisco to Camp Parks and we were in Camp Parks another couple of weeks awaiting the loading of our equipment on the SS Brazil, and set off then for Espiritu Santo in the Hebrides.

Q: This was a contained unit? You had all your equipment on board with you, and the men?

Capt. T.: And another battalion and their equipment. In other words, two battalions, about 2,200 men, and the equipment for both battalions.

Q: How large was the Brazil?

Capt. T.: She was about 6,000 tons, or something like that. Not a very large boat. To retrace my steps just a moment.

In the course of the loading, my commanding officer and I had made numerous inquiries of people we felt could give us some information about when we landed at some place, what was going to happen then. We were told that we would be unloaded by the shore forces, those who were there ahead of us.

Q: Were they Seabees, too?

Capt. T.: There were a lot of Seabees out by that time, of

course. We were the 57th Battalion. They said, however, that they planned to load our complement of pontoons on the deck and we determined that pontoons on the deck were fine, but we must be sure that all our necessary hardware was there. I had been involved in the development of the hardware for the pontoons and the Sea Horses - we called them Sea Horses - up in Davisville, so I knew more about pontoons than anybody did. My commanding officer didn't know a thing about them. I'd been in Davisville for a year, you see, and part of my job was the development of the gear that we were going to use abroad, whereas none of the other fellows had even seen it. They came right out of civilian life and started to learn how to march and so on, but they knew nothing about what equipment we were going to use.

Anyway, the upshot of it was that because I'd had this previous experience I saw to it that the necessary hardware, all the bolts and angles and clips and whatnot necessary to assemble the pontoons and rig the sea horses was available on deck.

We landed at Espiritu Santo early one morning and, not having been told, were hot to get ashore. Everybody was dressed, had their helmets on with their rifles over their shoulders. As we came into the harbor we were just fighting mad.

Q: How long had you been at sea?

Capt. T.: I've forgotten how long it took us. I think it was almost three weeks. She was a very slow ship. As we got there and rounded the point, we were asghast to find about ninety ships in the harbor, Segund Channel. We were greeted by the harbormaster's craft and told where to anchor and to stand by, that we would be visited. On short order a craft came alongside and the harbormaster's representative told us that we were in for a nice long wait, some of these ships had been in port for ninety days. They didn't have enough forces to unload nor enough equipment to unload. Then he said, we'll be mighty glad when you get ashore because I see you have pontoons here, which we lack sadly, but for the time being you'll just have to stay put.

This, of course, absolutely put a damp cloth on everybody. We were so crestfallen and hot and so dirty at that point. Everybody wanted to get ashore, but we were told positively that we couldn't go ashore because there was no place to house us or feed us or anything else.

Q: But you were a self-contained unit, couldn't you take care of yourselves?

Capt. T.: We were a self-contained unit and that's exactly what we wanted to do. So my commanding officer and I asked permission to go ashore - that was Lieutenant Commander Dwight P. Nardman. We went ashore in the harbormaster's craft and reported to Captain Andrew Bissett, CEC, USN, who was the commanding officer of the Seabees stationed on Espiritu Santo, all attached to so-called Lion 1.

Q: Lion 1 was a code name?

Capt. T.: Lion 1 was a code name for the island under Captain Jimmy Boak. So we reported to Captain Bissett. He was very glad to see us but repeated what the harbormaster had said, there was just no possibility of getting us ashore for umpty-umpty weeks, he could make no prediction, but he said, "We simply haven't got the barges or the personnel to unload the ships any faster than we're unloading them now. Also, most of the ships in the harbor are cargo ships, but there are a number of ships containing personnel that we can't get ashore."

So we said, "Would you mind, Captain, if we tried to help ourselves?" And he said, "Not at all. Anything you can do, do it." We went back to the ship and called a meeting of the officers to get organized. Our plan was to dump the pontoons over the side and assemble them in the water and take ourselves ashore. I think we started about noon on that day -

Q: This being the following day after you -

Capt. T.: No, this being the same day. We went ashore at seven o'clock or eight o'clock in the morning, by noon we were

3' x 7' pontoon barges such as assembled from deck of our ship to get two battalions ashore.

Pontoons dropped overboard from many ships and towed ashore for assembly. Most of hardware - angles, bolts, etc., were still in the holds of these ships and so the pontoons could not be assembled until the ships had been entirely unloaded.

back aboard and had made our plans, and started dumping pontoons overboard with ropes attached. Then we put some personnel on a couple of pontoons and fastened the first angles to the barges with the hardware that we now had at hand and we made what we called three by seven barges. In other words, they were seven pontoons long in one string and there were three strings, so it was called a three by seven barge. And we flipped it upside down, each string at a time, to put the four angles on the four corners until we had three individual strings made up, and then assembled the strings together with the clips and hardware that we had at hand, and then lowered one of the sea horses to it.

Q: How far were you standing offshore?

Capt. T.: Oh, we were offshore about a quarter of a mile. The sea horse, of course, is the forerunner of the present outboard engines, exactly the same principle. We had completed the assembly of the first barge by two o'clock in the morning. In other words, in about fourteen hours we had completed it. We had one in the water and it was ready to use. In the meantime, we had put enough pontoons in the water to assemble a second barge and that was in progress on the other side of the ship.

Q: Did you have to, in tropical waters, contend with underwater dangers, like sharks?

Capt. T.: There were no sharks down there. We never saw a shark. In fact, we had a hard time finding any fish at all. I'll come to that later.

Then we transferred our energies to the second barge and I think by eight o'clock we had two barges complete -

Q: Next morning?

Capt. T.: Eight o'clock next morning - and we started disembarking. We put all our people ashore and all the other battalion ashore, and then started on gear, on our housekeeping gear, tents and other things like that. So by eleven or twelve o'clock that day we went back to call on Captain Bissett and told him that we were ashore and where were we supposed to build our camp. He said, "You what" and I said, "Well, we, all our personnel, are ashore, Sir, and our housekeeping gear is following. We'll be ready to pitch camp this afternoon." He said, "I don't believe it," so rushed down to the waterfront and, sure enough, saw our people there on the shore! And the gear coming off the ship. Well, this was an absolute revelation, so he gave us a camp site and we pitched camp and got fairly well bedded down. It took one day to get ourselves in order and the day after that we reported for construction duty.

Triest #2 - 67

Q: There were other Seabee outfits there?

Capt. T.: There were about four other Seabee units there at that time.

Q: Why wasn't the captain able to learn from them that they were a little bit different in their approach to problems?

Capt. T.: I don't know. He was a civil engineer himself, of course, but I guess the reason was that no one had known what to expect. Their hardware for assembling these barges was in the holds of their ships, which is where ours was scheduled to be if we hadn't intervened and seen to it that our hardware was all on deck or we'd never have been able to make it. This was just the difference between a little bit of experience which I had had at Davisville and the fellows who had no experience. I was the only officer, I think, from Davisville who had gone out by that time. I think I was the first officer who was detached from Davisville to go out with the Seabees.

Q: Well, that was, again, quite an accomplishment!

Capt. T.: We set about our business and were consigned to various construction projects, I think probably about thirty-odd projects, in the first three weeks we were there.

Triest #2 - 68

Q: Was this all in connection with the ninety ships in the harbor?

Capt. T.: No, we had very little to do with that. The only assignment in that case was what we called the pontoon assembly depot, where we made the seven by nine barges. They were seven strings wide and nine pontoons long. These were 250-ton barges. They were the ones that were principally required to carry cargo ashore. We had enough pontoons with us to assemble three or four of these big barges as well as the two small ones. The smaller barges were used as towing barges to draft the big barges ashore. The only assignment that we had in connection with the unloading of the ships was, as I say, the development of and the maintenance of the pontoon assembly depot, and every pontoon that came off any of the ships was immediately given to us for assembly into these big cargo barges.

Q: This question is not very relevant to your story, but what about these ships containing personnel and being forced to

Triest #2 - 69

stay on board for a long period of time? Wasn't there illness?

Capt. T.: There wasn't very much illness because at that time they were still healthy. In other words, they had not been subjected to jungle rot and dysentery and other things that they soon got out there, and malaria. These were all state-side people and they were healthy enough so they could withstand periods of discomfort and lack of sanitation and so on. So it wasn't that serious at that point. It would have been very serious later on.

Q: Well, as to the other construction projects that were assigned to you during the first several weeks?

Capt. T.: We built, for example, an ammunition depot across Segund Channel, consisting of about twenty-five ammunition huts, and quarters for the personnel that were going to man the depot. We put our bulldozers, tractors and scrapers to work assigning some of them to so-called Fighter 1, which was a Marine fighter airstrip, and Bomber 3, which was an Army bomber strip. We built Captain Boak's headquarters, including messhalls and a theater for the island.

Q: How long had they been there?

Capt. T.: They had been there about eight or ten months, I

guess, at this point.

Q: It was awfully slow in getting their needs!

Capt. T.: Very slow, very slow indeed. The answer was lack of equipment, lack of building material, essentially wood and corrugated sheets, nails and so on. They were at a tremendous premium. Again, logistically, they didn't - nobody knew, nobody had had this experience, so that it was difficult to give proper priorities to the various materials that were necessary. Of course, the Navy lived entirely differently than the Army. The Army was better equipped for bivouacking. They were land people and they were used to pup tents and sleeping bags or blankets and cooking k-rations with a small fire where they could and moving day by day to another bivouac area.

The Navy had never been involved in anything of this kind before, and the Navy tradition of shipside comforts was carried forward to the shore, much to our pleasure, of course. We had sheets and pillows and refrigerators and housekeeping gear of all kinds that the Army and the Marines couldn't afford because it wasn't sufficiently mobile. We were intended to be set up in permanent bases where we could perform operational work. The only facilities that they did send out in complete fashion were hospitals, for example, and this was also part of my job. At Davisville we organized the complete complements for a surgical quonset, a messhall, a shower quonset, a mortuary, various and sundry specialized medical units, dentistry, x-ray, and so on. Each of these quonsets that went out went out with its full complement of gear. So when they arrived, it was simply a question of looking the numbers up on the various crates, assorting them, and then when we, as construction forces, started to build we found that Davisville had done its homework very well. We were able to set up a hospital in jig time and have it complete and ready for operation. Of course, these hospitals were the hospitals that took care of everybody, the Army and the Marines, and so on.

Q: They were separate from Red Cross units?

Capt. T.: The Red Cross units actually had nothing there. They had only a Red Cross director, generally a man with two or three girls for recreational purposes and for counseling purposes and that kind of thing. But they had absolutely no -

Q: No medical?

Capt. T.: No medical, no nothing. They simply aided and abetted the chaplains and tried to keep morale up and instituted what little recreational facilities were possible.

Q: In connection with hospitals and other needs, how did you provide electricity?

Capt. T.: We had our own generators. In other words, we had a full complement of gear, the most important of which, as I mentioned, was the refrigerator because the supply ships that came out came out well equipped with oranges and apples and eggs and meat and so on, and these refrigerators were, of course, a godsend because you couldn't keep anything in that broiling heat without refrigerator plants. In addition to that, one of the most necessary elements were the distillation units. We had a couple of sizes of distillation units - small ones for small groups and fairly decent-sized units to distill fresh water from salt water where fresh water was not available. On most of the islands, by judicious searching, we found sufficient fresh water for most of our needs, but on certain islands it was very difficult. The water was too brackish to drink. So a distillation unit was extremely important also for sanitation in galleys and so on.

Q: You say in some places you did find water. This was underground streams?

Capt. T.: Yes, and wells and so on.

Q: Was it not possible to use rain water? There was so much

Triest #2 - 73

of it.

Capt. T.: But we had very little equipment to gather it - the rain water. A lot of the boys did collect rain water, but it was not an easy thing to do. In the first place, the only materials available were khaki canvas-treated tents and rain water collected in that canvas was pretty miserable to try to drink. It was perfectly safe, but the chemicals that they treated the canvas with made the collection of water in that canvas very bad, and we had no untreated canvas at all.

Q: Was that not perhaps an oversight in equipment?

Capt. T.: It would have been done in another go-around, I'm sure, for the adequate collection of water. The truth of the matter is that you'd have to have a great big collection area to supply the needs of even one battalion of 1,100 men.

Q: Yes, and you did employ desalinization?

Capt. T.: In the areas where the battalions were on low-level islands like Tulagi, for example, Guadalcanal and Bougainville and so on, where the average height was only four or five feet above the water, it was difficult to get fresh water, so we had to rely on distilled water for cooking and drinking purposes.

Triest #2 - 74

Q: You spoke about one of your first jobs being building ammunition dumps and so forth, how did you protect the ammunition? How did you keep it dry?

Capt. T.: These were all shells and they didn't need to be kept dry. In other words, the old slogan about "keep your powder dry" was not necessary in this case. These shells all came ashore on pallettes and were trucked to the sites of the ammunition depots and stored there. Dryness was no problem.

Q: It was a problem in many ways, wasn't it?

Capt. T.: Oh, yes, but not from the point of view of ammunition. Another one of our jobs was the building of a degaussing station. The ships were paraded past this degaussing station in one of the channels so as to see that they had perfected as many demagnetization measures as they could, because, of course, all the mines were magnetic mines and the Navy went to great lengths to try to degauss ships by means of throwing cables around the ships and charging them with a voltage which would counteract the magnetization, the natural magnetization of the hull.

Q: How did this magnetization develop over the ship?

Capt. T.: I frankly don't know. That's not my business and I know very little about it.

Q: But it does happen.

Capt. T.: It does happen, yes.

Q: I noticed in the story of the 57th that there's a picture of the degaussing operation on a separate island.

Capt. T.: That's right. A small island just off Segund Channel, Capintu Santo.

Q: Was there any reason for that, separating it from the other operations?

Capt. T.: I think only because the coral slope was such that we could operate rather easily, because, for the most part, the drop-off was quite severe, and in this case we had to install underwater equipment. It was easier to do it on a sloping beach rather than - you couldn't do it on a sheer surface because the water sometimes dropped off 20 or 30 feet from the edge of the coral reef right straight down. In other cases, we had broad reaches of coral, sandy coral, that we could operate on.

Q: You might tell me about one of the major operations, and

that was the runways for airplanes, you mentioned them, but some of the problems involved in doing this, clearing the jungle, and keeping it clear, dealing with the mud, laying down marston mats, and so forth?

Capt. T.: This was one of those things that had to evolve. The situations at each location were quite similar, yet dissimilar. Generally speaking, of course, the islands were covered with very, very heavy forestry, banyan trees, and other trees in profusion with roots that were very extensive. In other words, it'd be nothing to find a tree that would have a root - a multitude of roots coming out maybe fifty feet. Of course, this is where we couldn't have gotten along without our tractors. We had International Harvester D-8s and Caterpillar D-8 tractors. The clearing of an airstrip was a very, very horrendous program, and of course that was the first thing to be done. Then we pulled scraper pans behind these tractors to level the ground. When we'd get to coral, generally speaking, the scrapers could pick up the so-called loose coral, or coral that had not been too solidified - if I may use that word for lack of a better one at the moment. When we came to the tough coral of course, we had to use a power shovel or, in some cases, dynamite.

Q: The loose coral was -

Triest #2 - 77

Capt. T.: That was usually topsoil, almost topsoil, just under the surface where the material was not as solidified as it was further down.

But for the most part, as I say, we had to either use shovels or bulldozers and just loosen it so that the scrapers could pick it up and transport it to grade the runways.

Q: How deep a foundation did you have to have for a runway?

Capt. T.: We generally didn't need any foundation because the surface material, being coral, was sufficiently hard so that we didn't need any foundation, as such. In other words, if we, say, excavated four feet in one spot and took that four feet of material and put it in a low spot, then the running back and forth of the equipment was enough to compact it. And then topping it off with the road-scrapers so that we could get a proper grade for water drainage. We found that if we didn't grade properly and the water during a rainstorm settled in any one spot, then it got very, very mushy. In other words, the coral became saturated and very mushy. But it we graded it so the rain ran right off, it got almost as hard as concrete.

Q: Did you do any tiling to accomplish this? Putting tiles down to drain off the rain?

Capt. T.: No, we had no tiles. It was simply a question of putting a proper crown on the runway and grading it from - in one direction, so that we would not have any low spots. The same thing with roads. When we built roads we always tried to keep a high crown on the road, because as soon as you got down to a level grade, then within a matter of hours, you'd have just the biggest mud hole you've ever seen. If we could get away from the mud, the topsoil, and replace it with coral and build it up to a point where it had proper drainage, we had perfectly lovely roads, wonderful.

Q: I suppose the materials we're most accustomed to like macadam and concrete don't stand up too well in 120 inches of rain?

Capt. T.: We couldn't get that material out there, Number One. So we had to use the coral and coral is an excellent building material, and as long as we had equipment to keep the ruts out of it and keep it graded, it was perfect. The fighter strips and the bomber strips necessarily had to be good. We had no trouble at all in that respect. In certain other places where the average level above the water was so low, places where there was only three or four feet above water, the whole subsurface was spongy. Then we used landing mats in profusion. But in Espiritu Santo we were quite high above the water, maybe twenty-five or thirty feet, so we had a different situation there.

Q: Did you have any special problems with the disposal of the debris, the tree trunks and all the jungle growth that you had to clear out?

Capt. T.: We burned it.

Q: You had to burn it. And what about the enemy seeing these as beacons?

Capt. T.: Well, the enemy knew we were there and Washing Machine Charlie, our Japanese spy, came over every night, and he knew we were there. There's no doubt about that. We never burned anywhere near a camp and, of course, the airfields under construction were - there was nothing there, so there was nothing for them to attack. In fact, I don't think we had any enemy attacks while we were on Espiritu Santo. We were too far from the fighting front. The fighting front, at that time, was up around Guadalcanal, which was about 700 miles to the north of us. We didn't see any fighter planes around Espiritu Santo.

Q: They merely sent planes to observe?

Capt. T.: That's right.

Q: How did you keep the clearing under jungle conditions, where it grows so fast?

Capt.: That's true, but once the coral had been denuded of topsoil and had been compacted and graded so that the water didn't stand there, we had practically no trouble with new growth coming up through the coral. In the first place, we had to run our graders back and forth two or three times a week in order to keep it level and smooth and free from ruts, so any growth that did spring up through the coral was quickly eradicated. That was no problem.

Q: Was it a problem with the marston mats?

Capt. T.: I wasn't associated with any matting operations and I therefore don't know.

While we were on Espiritu Santo, we had one very interesting experience when Eleanor Roosevelt and Mrs. Grace Ritchie, two very striking women, came out on a morale junket. The place was in a flurry. They were to be housed in Admiral Boak's compound. We had taken existing quonsets and devised some curtains and built special johns and other things so that they could be comfortable and be protected. They spent a couple or three days there and did a tremendous amount to boost the morale of the boys.

Q: What did she do?

Triest #2 - 81

Capt. T.: As I recall, she spoke to the boys at the theater one night. This was sort of a little encouraging type of talk. I'm very vague at this stage as to exactly what she said or what her tone was, but it was sort of a "get on with the show, boys" type of talk and extremely well received by everybody and a great morale booster. We had seen no females at that point at all, and even though these ladies were untouchable they were still females!

Q: I suppose she inspected everything.

Capt. T.: Oh, yes, naturally, and discussed everything with everybody, asked how they were getting along.

Q: Yes, I remember the publicity on that.

Capt. T.: And then we were visited also by two or three USO troupes. I'll tell you about one interesting experience on Emirau later on when I get to that.

Q: What kind of entertainment did you have on Espiritu Santo?

Capt. T.: We had movies every night. We'd get the films from the ships and trade them back and forth. Each ship had a supply of ten or twelve or fifteen movies and they had their printed lists of what movies they had and so on, so there was a free interchange of movies between ships and shore establishments. A lot of them came directly to us via planes and, as I say, we had a movie every night. And whenever the USO troupes came they had comedians or they had music or dancing or something of that kind, and they generally carried a couple or three girls with them, and those were the first gals that we'd seen. Later on, of course, the Red Cross girls came. Red Cross girls came to establish recreational facilities. Then there were some Army nurses, of course, at that time, too.

Q: Did the backlog of shipping in the harbor decrease as a result of the presence of this very energetic Seabee outfit?

Capt. T.: We had with us what we called the 6th Seabee Special outfit which was in those days called a negro battalion, a stevedore battalion, now they would be called "black". And the blacks were specially organized - they had been recruited from stevedore units in this country, the same as the Seabees had been recruited from construction people. The stevedores knew their business and they shouldered the great responsibility of unloading the cargo as well as personnel. They were bivouaced right next to us.

I'll never forget a Commander Yost of the Coast Guard - a lieutenant commander in those days - who was the commanding officer of the 6th Seabee Special. In other words, the specials were the stevedores and that was the 6th. How many

Triest #2 - 83

more there were of this type of battalion, I don't know.

Q: Did your outfit have anything to do with setting up a repair base for shipping?

Capt. T.: I'll come to that later, when we get to Guadalcanal and Tulagi.

Q: Not on Santo?

Capt. T.: Not on Santo.

Q: They did have some?

Capt. T.: They did have some and, as a matter of fact, we did the preliminary work. When I was there we were just starting the erection of facilities that were later to be used for ship repairs, including a floating dry dock that had been taken through the canal - turned on edge and taken through the canal - and towed out to Espiritu Santo. I had gone by that time.

Q: You were actually there, what length of time?

Capt. T.: I was there a year. In the latter part of this year, I suppose after we'd been there about eight months, a very interesting episode occurred.

It had been the practice all through the island areas that whenever a bridge was built it was built by the Army according to routine old-time construction design. That is, driving piles, made from the trees that were cut down, on bents every fourteen feet and x-bracing so that they would be selfsufficient and then decking was put on top for bridging purposes. Of course, these went across the various rivers that emanated from the centers of the islands. Every time there was a big storm, tremendous amounts of debris would be floated down the rivers and because of a bridge being there it would dam up on the bridge. The instance that I want to describe now occurred on a river where the water rose eleven feet behind this dam held by the bridge. Of course, the bridge wasn't designed for that purpose and so it collapsed. This had happened two or three times during the eight months that the island had been occupied before we got there. Captain Bissett decided that this time we'd do it differently. We would build a steel bridge.

So we took three 105-foot strings of pontoons and floated them up the river to the site of the bridge. Meantime, other forces were removing the debris from the dam that had collected behind the bridge before it collapsed and cleaned it out, so that future rains could carry it downriver. We established two strong abutments about 80 feet apart so as to give a clear space of eighty feet for the water to traverse. Then the

Original Saraka River Bridge - Espititu Santo.

Original Saraka River Bridge

strings of pontoons were lifted and placed on top of the abutments three strings wide to form a permanent bridge.

When this project was started, the 71st Battalion under Lieutenant Commander Wendt and the 57th and one or two other battalion people were called into consultation with Captain Bissett who layed out his plan for building this bridge and determine which was the best battalion to do the job. I wanted to get it for out battalion, the 57th, very much because I had been in the steel erection business all my life building subways before the war, therefore I knew something about the steel business. But Commander Wendt was a very forceful individual and he had a chief petty officer who was a steel erection foreman. He was able to sell the job for his battalion.

Every battalion had a three-quarter yard Koehring crane and it was necessary to have two cranes on this job in order to life the strings of pontoons out of the water and put them on the abutments. So he said to the 57th Battalion, "You give your crane to Commander Wendt to supplement his and supply him with whatever else he may need." It developed, however, that his own forces had enough experience and enough men available to do all the construction work of the abutments and so on, and therefore we only had to supply a crane and an operator.

When the day came to erect - to take the first string of pontoons out of the water and place it on the abutments, for which a crane was needed at either abutment, the chief petty officer in charge stood in the middle of the string and signaled with both hands to the operators of the cranes on either side. Of course, he could only look in one direction at one time, and so they raised the pontoon string successfully while he was standing in the middle. Then he gave his signals to turn, watching one side, but he obviously couldn't watch the other side simultaneously. And the moment he gave his signal, the operator on the far bank from ours, who was a highly nervous individual, immediately put his crane into what we called "swing gear" to swing the boom around and our operator started to do the same thing. Our man was an older man and a much more cautious operator and realizing that he had a considerable weight on his line - these strings weighed 33 tons each - in other words, each crane had to lift 16 1/2 tons - moved more cautiously. We had our booms fairly high so that we had about 18 feet, I think, from the centerline of the cranes to the centerline of the hoisting cable. That 18 feet was quite a momentum arm. Our operator started swinging at the same time or seconds after the other operator because he was faster. They didn't swing in unison. In other words, the first operator swung his a little too fast and he got the 33-ton weight going too fast and when it started to swing it was impossible to stop it and as it swung, it increased the distance from the centerline of our crane to the cable from 18 feet to 24 feet, or something of the kind, and the crane was pulled off the abutment into the water, about 16 or 18 feet, with the crane operator in the cab.

Of course, the end of the string that our crane was holding fell down into the water so that the string was resting, at that point, at about a 45-degree angle. The other crane was able to maintain its position because the string had been shoved nearer to the center of gravity of that machine and farther away from ours.

Fortunately, the operator wasn't hurt seriously and was able to extricate himself from the cab. This is the older man, the 57th man. They rushed him to the hospital and fortunately he only had a slight concussion of the head.

I had been standing downstream on the Army low-level pontoon type of bridge that the Army had to put across the river to serve as a temporary crossing. The captain and I and Commander Hardman, my commanding officer, and a lot of the Army brass and Navy brass were all there to watch this operation. Captain Bissett flew off the handle at that point and said that our operator was at fault because he had lowered his boom rather than swinging when he had been given the command to swing. He stalked off and went back to his headquarters.

Of course, I was immensely concerned not only for the sake of the man, but to have this accusation against us. It really hurt me as I felt in my heart that this was not true. I knew the man, he was an excellent operator, a very, very

1st Pontoon string tumbles

Completed pontoon bridge

capable man, and I knew that this couldn't have been. In any event, I sent my equipment officer to the hospital to talk to him as soon as it was possible and ask specifically whether he had changed his gears. There's a change level on the lefthand side of the operator, the cab being on the right-hand side of the machine. That level goes up and down, and if the level is in the down position it means that the crane, when activated by the control level, will swing, and if the lever is in the up position, it means that when the control level is activated, the boom will lower or raise. But you can't do the two things at one time. You cannot swing and lower or raise the boom simultaneously - one or the other. And what the captain had said was that our operator had lowered the boom, rather than swinging on command.

This was what we wanted to find out, whether there was any possibility that our operator had changed from swing to boom, and we found out that he positively had not. Then it flashed through my mind that the side of the cab was probably crushed in to such a degree that it would have precluded the movement of the shift lever.

When my equipment officer came back and gave us this report, I decided the only way to find out for sure was to send a diver down to examine the cab and see the position of the swing boom lever. He dove down and when he surfaced he reported that it was in swing position and it could not be any other way, the side of the cab having been crushed in which shoved the pedestal for the seat so tight against the wall that it was physically impossible to move the lever.

Well, the captain had called a conference in his headquarters about an hour and a half after the accident, and we went up to talk about it. In the meantime, I found this thing out. The captain reiterated his stand, and I said, "I beg your pardon, Captain, I don't believe that this is the fact. We've interrogated the operator in the hospital personally. He was able to talk to us and said positively he swung and he had not changed his swing-boom lever. Subsequently we went a diver down and he examined the cab and reports that the side of the cab is crushed in to a degree that it would be impossible to change it."

"Oh," he said, "I don't believe that. I think you've changed the gears."

I said, "Captain, we'll have the crane out of the water by six o'clock tonight and you can see for yourself."

There continued to be quite an altercation. He wasn't going to believe what we said. He had made up his mind and that was that. This was quite a serious charge. Anyway, by six o'clock the crane was out of the water and the captain was there watching it, and when it came out of the water, we demonstrated to him that beyond a doubt the man had told the truth and that the lever could not have been moved while our diver had been underwater because of the squeezed-in position of the cab.

So that was that and we repaired the machine, and the bridge was completed and so on.

About a month later the captain came into our camp one day and beckoned to me and said, where's Commander Hardman. Commander Hardman was in his tent at that moment. He was suffering from dysentery. The captain asked us to come over, so we went into the battalion headquarters which was another tent we used for that purpose, and he said, "Commander, can you spare Triest?" And the commander said, "If you say so, certainly." "Well," he said, "I tell you. I've got a tough situation up in Guadalcanal and Tulagi where the 27th Battalion has actually fallen to pieces and unless I can get them straightened out, we're going to have to send them home and we cannot afford to. We need manpower desperately for construction purposes, particularly as we advance."

Q: Bissett had jurisdiction over them, too?

Capt. T.: Yes. In fact, he had jurisdiction over all of the battalions in the South Pacific. He went on to describe the situation and asked me whether I'd like to take it, and I could hardly wait! So he said, "Well, I tell you, they started out with 1,100 officers and men, as you did. They've been out here two years and they are shipped. Eighty-five percent of them are on sick call. They're not doing any work. They look like the greatest rag-tag bunch of people you've ever seen with beards, Japanese uniforms, and unhealthy living conditions, foxholes full of water, beer cans all over the place. It's a perfect disgrace. The battalion has had five commanding officers in the last two years, and each one has proven worse than the last and has had to be relieved. Here we are with a situation where I need these men desperately and I haven't time to get another outfit out from the States, but if I can't straighten this one out, they'll have to go. I think you can do it."

I said, "I'd surely like to try." He said, "You have my blessing. Any officers that you want to replace, you have my sanction. Send me a secret dispatch and tell me what you want and it will be granted. And any other measures that you need to take, you just tell me." (At that time he had moved to Moumea). "And we will do it. I'd like a written report from you in the course of the next month whether you're going to be able to get this outfit in shape or not, so that we will know how to plan."

I thanked him and left that evening by plane for Guadalcanal and arrived in the most horrendous rainstorm you've ever seen. You couldn't see fifteen feet ahead of yourself. Just horrendous! The regimental commander of the 18th Regiment, Commander W. W. Studdert, from New Bern, North Carolina, met me at the plane, took me to his quarters because I was then assigned to him under the 18th Regiment. He dried me off and gave me a drink to warm me up a bit. At that time, it was freezing cold, even though it was on the equator, but these rainstorms and high winds cool you off in a hurry. I was really chattering, I was so cold.

Anyway, the next morning I went by boat to Tulagi where the battalion was encamped and found that the battalion was broken up into five or six encampments at different locations. As I approached the camp I saw Lieutenant William F. E. Cabaniss from Atlanta, Georgia, who was the executive officer. I asked for the commanding officer and he said, "Well, Commander Puls is out on one of the jobs. He'll be back shortly." So I said, "I suppose I should wait, but you probably know that I've come as his relief." He said, "Yes, we've heard, just this morning."

Anyway, Commander Puls came and, of course, he was crestfallen at the news that he was being relieved and being sent back to the States.

Q: He'd been there only a short time?

Capt. T.: He'd been there a matter of four or five months. Let me digress just a moment.

In the beginning, the only big mistake that was made when forming battalions was that they chose commanding officers, all lieutenant commanders, from the ranks of the Civil Engineer Corps. These men had been purposely brought into the Corps for Seabee purposes and were all what I would call "desk engineers," - design engineers of one kind or another or project managers in civilian life, but very few of them had any construction experience as contractors. They were mostly project or construction supervisors, and there's a great deal of difference.

Q: They'd never had any actual command of men?

Capt. T.: That is correct, exactly what I'm getting to. On the other hand, the Corps had wisely chosen to select executive officers from the ranks of construction people, and inevitably the executive officers assumed the command of the battalion once it had been determined that the commanding officer was not qualified to handle personnel. With no exceptions that I've heard of, were the construction people ever found deficient in their particular selection, but in every instance the book or design engineers were faulty and were replaced and sent back to the States or given some administrative job in the islands that required that type of thinking and that type of experience rather than the actual handling of personnel.

Unfortunately, Commander Puls was one of these design engineers, a very capable fellow and a very nice fellow, but that was not his particular forte. Anyway, we had to wait two or three days for his orders to come - to be received - so I made myself busy inspecting the various installations.

Triest #2 - 94

They were building a tank farm at so-called Marker D. which was a very fine harbor within the island of Tulagi. It had ninety feet of water or something of the sort and the battalion was building a fueling station there consisting of half a dozen 1000 barrel fuel-oil tanks and pipelines and whatnot, to fuel ships -

Q: May I ask you if you built a tank farm on Espiritu Santo as well?

Capt. T.: No. The first tank farm was at Marker D on Tulagi.

Q: May I ask one other question? The physical situation, the weather and what have you, was somewhat similar, was it not? All tropical?

Capt. T.: Except that at Espiritu Santo we experienced an average rainfall of about 120 inches, and in Tulagi there was an average rainfall of 330 inches!

Q: That is a difference!

Capt. T.: But we soon got so that the rain didn't bother us at all. In fact, it was welcome because it cooled us off and whenever we weren't working in the mud, everything was fine. In other words, steel erection in the rain was no problem and many of the other jobs -

Q: So long as you could see!

Capt. T.: As long as you could see, and you'd get soaking wet in a rainstorm that would last fifteen or twenty minutes, and then you'd be completely dry half an hour after. So it really made no difference and it helped to clean us!

Anyway, Commander Puls's orders finally came. I had a short meeting with the officers at that time and then called a meeting with the whole battalion the next morning at eight o'clock. That was quite an experience.

Q: How many men were involved?

Capt. T.: There were theoretically 1,120 men, and officers. I think probably that number had been reduced through sickness to about 900 at that point. I started to say they were building a tank farm at Marker D, a pontoon-assembly depot, a PT base at Lion Point, a hospital at Hulavo, and one or two other outpost installations. This was the first time I was acting on my own completely and, in the face of the data that I'd been given, I realized, having had three days to observe the conditions, what a really horrendous job it was going to be.

The first thing I had to do was to tell the men that they

were not going to go home, that we were going to go forward.

Q: And they'd been out how long?

Capt. T.: They'd been out two years, and the 26th Battalion had come out with them, and the 26th Battalion had, a month before, been sent home for rest and rehabilitation, so our boys felt there was no question that they were more than deserving of this, particularly when their record of illness was such and the morale was at such a low point.

I soon found out that I had to make a number of changes, including the chaplain, the doctor, five company commanders, and a couple of other officers. In other words, I think there were some twelve or fourteen officers that I recommended be replaced, and in each case I advanced the second in command of the company, whom I found to be excellent men, and I got a new doctor and a new chaplain.

They had sent a Catholic chaplain out with the battalion and the battalion was ninety-five percent Protestant. Of course, this didn't help. And it developed that the doctor was, let's say, far from abstemious, and that didn't help.

Q: Three hundred inches of rain didn't help either!

Capt. T.: That didn't help, plus the fact that whenever they transferred a man out for malaria reasons - and we had some very, very serious cases of malaria - the island commander sent him right back to us. (The island was under the command of the Army.) This had happened as many as four or five times to many of these boys, and some of them were desperately ill from malaria and fungus. So the subject of another dispatch to Captain Bissett was that when we sent a man out for illness, it was genuine, it would have my certification, and I felt that word had to be gotten back to the island commander that these men were to be returned to the States and not sent back to us because we couldn't function with a bunch of people who were almost too sick to stand on their feet. So, somehow or other, he got that word through, and the next time we shipped them out - we shipped out about forty men - they went home. We got replacements from the receiving camps.

At that time, all the volunteers had been used up and we had to take men out of the regular Navy ranks and make Seabees of them.

Anyway, to return to my meeting with the battalion. I started out by telling them that, unfortunately, they couldn't go home and we had to get ready to go forward. There was a very important job for us to do, and there was only one way to do it and that was to get with it and jump in with both feet. And, I said, I'm going to take whatever measures are necessary to evacuate the men that are truly sick, but those men that are malingering are going to get on the line and work, or there are going to be some courts-martial. I said as far our living conditions are concerned, the camp has to be gotten in shape. We're going to have a full-scale inspection tomorrow of all the facilities, including bedding, sanitation facilities, messhalls, foxholes, and the uniforms, and your appearance - you'll shave off all beards - discard all Japanese uniforms. You will draw proper naval uniforms from the supply depot here, and if you can't get it here we'll get it out of Guadalcanal. We're going to get ourselves in shape.

So we had an inspection the next morning. Of course, by this time I was absolutely soaking wet, just soaking wet. I deliberately placed myself facing the sun and the men with their backs to it, so aside from the anxiety and excitement of this speech, the realization of what I was telling these men was really an emotional experience. So that was that, and the next morning -

Q: How did they receive it?

Capt. T.: With groans, which you could hear from here to breakfast, but this soon died down.

The next morning things got ever worse because area by area, with the various commanders of each company, we went through with a couple of yeomen following us and taking notes -

Q: These were the old commanders still? They hadn't been

replaced?

Capt. T.: The old commanders, right. We went through the various quarters and said this will be corrected and that will be corrected. What's this man's name, and so on, and I want you to put all these men on notice that these infractions have got to be corrected.

Q: Had there been extensive shaving overnight?

Capt. T.: There had been considerable shaving and some of the foxholes had been cleaned up but not to any great extent. And I said, we'll have another inspection in five days and by that time I expect to see things put to right. By the end of that day I had made up my mind that we would never have any unity developed within the battalion while we were scattered in the five or six camps where these boys were living and acting almost as they pleased. In other words, there was no central command and there were no facilities and they were living under the most horrendous conditions.

Q: Did you discover why this had come about?

Capt. T.: Because of the nature of the land. In other words, if you've ever examined a map of Tulagi, which I will give you, you will see that the various facilities were just too far apart to bring the men back to camp every night, and in order to get anything out of them they had to live where they were working. To bring the men back from Marker D - the fueling station they were building - to the main camp and back again, aside from not having enough water transportation, would have taken probably an hour each way.

So I decided that night that the only way to do was to move the battalion to Guadalcanal and get them under one roof, so to speak, in one camping area. This would give us a chance to get ready to go forward as I'd found out through the scuttlebutt that the move that they were priming us for was to take place in about a month's time. Our move, incidentally, wasn't going to leave a lot of loose ends as the major projects, including the fueling stations, had for all intents and purposes, been completed.

Q: Then the distance from Tulagi -

Capt. T.: To Guadalcanal was about eight miles.

Before telling you about our move to Guadalcanal, however, I think I would like to recite some experiences that the boys had before I got there because these were really quite extraordinary. One of the reasons that the battalion had been kept there is because they had done some very good work in this area, which was ship repair. There were no Navy ship-repair facilities north of Espiritu Santo at that time. This was in the year that I was in Espiritu Santo. There were some ship-repair facilities working there but to no great extent. All the serious damage had to go back to San Francisco.

In the meantime, in this year's time, we had some very, very fine people and they just, without any prodding, had taken it upon themselves, the individual company officers, to pick up and do something, and when a ship came in that was in dire need of repair, either hull repair or propeller change, or something that they couldn't handle they sent frantic messages ashore to the commander of the naval base, whose name was "Scrappy" Kessing - Captain "Scrappy" Kessing - for help, and the 27th was the only facility that he could turn to to afford that help. As a result, in a year's time, our boys performed ship repairs of one kind or another on about 450 vessels, including the changing of propellers on 120 of them. And the changing of propellers had to be undertaken by men wearing gas masks that they converted to diving masks. They got their oxygen from compressors into the hose lines through home made filters to filter out the compressor oil. They made filters out of bales of cotton and stuffed them into the tubes and took the relatively clean air from the outboard side of these filters to give them air to work under water.

They also built their own underwater cutting torches to cut the nuts off the shafts to permit removal of the propellers. All this done under water. They'd cut the nut off and then they'd put an eighth of a stick of dynamite 180° apart on the back side of each propeller, and blow the whole propeller off and install a new one. Most of the ships carried spare propellers, fortunately.

And they did all kinds of other work, myriad numbers of jobs. The boys had set up a complete machine shop on shore and were able to do machine work that the ships couldn't perform themselves. In one instance we had an LCI limp into Tulagi which had been used on the Bougainville invasion. They had ripped 105 feet of the 120 feet of their starboard tanks going across a coral reef. When the ship limped into Tulagi she was heeled over about 42°. Nobody knows yet how she got in. And as they came into port, three of our boys were on our work boat and the captain hailed them and asked what they should do with her and, with very quick thinking, the chief took command and said, "Throw us a line and we'll guide you." They brought the boat around so that it was breeched - heeled outboard - along the shore at Hulago and quietly settled there. The crew got off and that was that.

The next day our boys attached three bulldozers to her and by the aid of snatch blocks to trees on the shore, were able to right the boat into position. Then the divers went down and examined the ruptured tanks, and they found that the plates had been buckled in where she had gone over the coral reef but they decided that they could fix it. So, by cutting wedges and using a lot of burlap, they formed plugs and actually plugged the holes from the outside to make it sufficiently watertight so that the boat could be de-watered. They pumped the boat out, steamed out the fuel tanks so that they could work inside, and then, taking plates that they cut from the Japanese sawmills on shore, welded a framework inside to cover these ruptures. The welding in these tanks was under frightful conditions - it must have been $140°$ in the tanks, I don't know how they stood it. In eleven days the ship was ready for sea.

Q: With such a record, when did they begin to be a do-nothing battalion?

Capt. T.: This type of work was being done by a few men, maybe twenty or twenty-five men, who were doing a wonderful job, but the rest of them were just - and there were another twenty-five or fifty out at Marker D erecting the fuel tanks. But the other jobs that they were doing were just of no account. And that was what led me to request that the battalion be moved to Guadalcanal. The ship work only came in one ship at a time or two ships at a time and actually when I took over there was no ship work in progress, and the tank farm had been 95% completed, so that it wasn't necessary to leave any men there to finish that job.

We moved the battalion to Guadalcanal and set up camp there and with the experience that I had had on Espiritu

Santo Santo decided we'd lay the new camp out in a prearranged very orderly fashion. We put the tents in neat rows and we set up our messhall, with screening and we built sterilization units consisting of water that we could boil, using homemade oil-burner equipment, so that every man had a sterile mess tray. We went to great lengths to eradicate the flies and mosquitoes to eliminate dysentery and further infection of malaria and so on.

Q: Did the boys enter into this with enthusiasm?

Capt. T.: Oh, with great enthusiasm, great. Then it was discovered that this scuttlebutt that I had heard that we were going to go forward in a month was not correct, but as a result of my reports to Captain Bissett to the effect that we were ready to go or would be ready to go shortly and because the next move had been postponed for two months, two and a half months, we suddenly got orders to take us to New Zealand for a month of rest and rehabilitation. We'd gotten ourselves in pretty darn good shape at that point, but they still needed rest. In other words, their health had improved and the replacements that were being received had rebuilt the morale, but we needed a rest. So we were ordered to Auckland, New Zealand.

Q: This must have helped morale?

Capt. T.: It helped tremendously, tremendously.

Interview #3 with Captain Willard G. Triest

Place: His office in Annapolis, Maryland

Date: Wednesday afternoon, 26 July 1972

Subject: Biography

By: John T. Mason, Jr.

Q: It's good to see you. Last time, you were talking about the move to Tulagi and the rebuilding of esprit de corps in the outfit there. You told me about a few of the projects undertaken and then had wound up with the fact that you were being sent for rest and relaxation to New Zealand for a month. However, before you went to New Zealand, there were other projects which you should include in this story, so do you want to resume at that point?

Capt. T.: Yes, I think I should revert to Tulagi and tell you a little bit about some of the things that the boys had accomplished at Tulagi other than those projects which I've already recited.

For example, the Seabees being what they are, you couldn't keep them down and even though they were working twelve hours a day there was still plenty of time when they had little to do. Entertainment was practically nil at that stage and so they inevitably got involved in other things. For example, any number of them helped the Army man anti-aircraft positions at night.

Q: This was a volunteer thing?

Capt. T.: It was completely volunteer, right. On one occasion there was an antiaircraft position right outside of our main camp, within 400 or 500 yards of the entrance to Tulagi Harbor. One of our boys was helping to man an antiaircraft position but at that particular point was not on the gun but he had a 30/30 rifle, and a kamikaze came down aimed directly at the ships that were fueling off of Marker D, which was the fueling harbor of Tulagi. The antiaircraft guns let loose on this kamikaze to no effect, apparently, but this chap of ours, whose name escapes me at the moment, fired <u>one</u> shot from his 30/30 and the plane went down. The next day they recovered it from 90 feet of water and found that the bullet had gone right through the man's temple - one bullet from a 30/30. Quite an extraordinary thing.

Q: Marksmanship!

Capt. T.: Yes, and, of course, you don't know how much it may have saved in the way of ships damaged because this man was loaded with explosives and aiming right for four or five ships that were anchored in the harbor.

Then, on any number of other occasions, for example, the boys manned PT boats operating out of Tulagi, mostly as a thrill.

Triest #3 - 108

Q: What were those missions?

Capt. T.: These were missions of the PT boats against the enemy up in Bougainville and Green and some of the islands - and Munda - most of Tulagi. They had some really extraordinary experiences in the battles that went on in the channel between Guadalcanal and Tulagi.

Q: That was called The Slot, wasn't it?

Capt. T.: The Slot, but I can't think of the name of it. Actually these islands were Rendova, and New Georgia, and Kula Gulf, and Vella Lavella, and Treasury were all north and west of Tulagi.

Q: These efforts on the part of your men over and above the ordinary duties of the day would seem to underscore the revived spirit which they had?

Capt. T.: No. As I said, this happened before I took over. In other words, it was during the first two years of their occupancy and before they had become so badly off physically that they became dis-spirited. This was in the earlier stages and during the thick of the fighting. Actually, by the time I took over the fighting had been completely finished.

Triest #3 - 109

Q: At Henderson Field on Guadalcanal and around there?

Capt. T.: Right. The only fighting that was going on at that time was in the islands north and west of Guadalcanal, Munda and Vella Lavella, and Bougainville, and Green Island. At that point I received permission to take the battalion to Guadalcanal and, for the first time, built a sensible camp, predesigned, rather than built by happenstance, and within a matter of a few days we were all standing colors morning and night and the men were dressed in proper uniform and the spirit was rising very rapidly, aided and abetted, of course, by the fact that by that time I had been able to have the very sick men evacuated. Their places had been taken by others sent to us who were in good health, so that really lifted the spirits of the whole organization.

Q: Did you get an immediate reaction from the captain who was in overall charge?

Capt. T.: Oh, without question yes. He was extremely pleased and, as a result, assigned us to the next mission, largely on my reports that - of what had been done, and on Commander Studdard's recommendation that we were ready to go forward.

Q: You mentioned off-tape several different projects in which the men engaged. For instance, the building of the headquarters for Admiral Aubrey Fitch. Do you want to tell me about that?

Capt. T.: That was really a mundane construction job. We simply built a number of huts for his headquarters and an entertainment center, or theater, and cleared quite a respectable area, but there was nothing spectacular about that.

After we'd been on Guadalcanal a couple of weeks, I guess, we had a very, very severe storm and every time one of these storms occurred on Guadalcanal, as in the other islands, bridges that had been built were, for the most part, washed away through debris coming down from the highlands. In this particular case, the Nalimbu River bridge was washed away and by this time the island command was very desperate because every time these bridges were washed away the progress of the war virtually came to a halt. Everything on Guadalcanal was located on the southwest coast and there was just the one road.

Q: You didn't have any other options?

Capt. T.: There were no other options, so when this storm came and washed this bridge out Commander Studdard called several of the battalion commanders to his headquarters to discuss the situation. I suggested that we ought to build a steel bridge out of pontoons, rather than try to rebuild the old wooden structure, of which many had been built in the previous years.

Q: And they'd suffered the same fate?

Capt. T.: Right. And he said, "I don't know where you're going to get the pontoons. We just haven't any of that sort of equipment here on the island." I said, "Well, there's one five-by-seven string that we've noticed outside our camp at Lunga Point. This barge apparently was sunk on the original invasion. It was riddled with holes and was three-quarters covered with sand and water, but, "I think we can salvage it. If we can get it ashore, then I think we can transport it the seven miles up the coast to the Nalimbu River, and we'll put a bridge across much the same as we did down in the Hebrides, only in this case we won't be able to bring it up the stream. The stream in the normal season has only four or five inches of water in spots, it's mostly pebbles and rocks. But we can take it over the land and my plan would be to catapult it across the stream."

So he gaveus permission to do it and his blessing and we started in that afternoon. I employed about 115 men, I think it was, around the clock. We first stripped away the debris that had collected in front of the old piers and cleared the old pilings out. Then we built two strong abutments with an 80-foot clear span across this river. Next we went ashore

Bridges like this over the Nalimbu River were washed out every storm

A salvaged string from a pontoon barge used on the invasion of Gudalcanal. The sag was removed when the string was welded to make a girder of it so that it could support heavy road traffic.

A dry run to see whether we could actually cantilever this 107 foot string across an 80 foot clear span.

Last four pontoons are filled with water to effect the necessary counterbalance.

Cantilevering a 107 foot string across an 80 foot clear span.

Turning the strings from a 5 foot wide by 7 foot deep section to a 7 foot wide by 5 foot deep section to make a 21 foot wide bridge (see article in appendix).

Finished bridge supports a 45 ton load and deflects only .1 feet at center. The string on top is for the next bridge on Route 1.

off our camp and by virtue of using our underwater cutting equipment that we had developed, cut the strings apart so that we could bring one string ashore at a time. A lot of these pontoons had been so badly punctured that they were full of sand and we had to use pumps to pump water in to pump sand out, or flush the sand out to make them light enough to handle.

In any event, while one gang was working on the salvage of these pontoons, the rest of the force was working on the bridge abutments in preparation. We used some rear axles and wheels from some of our equipment and loaded the strings on these transporters and did transport the strings the seven miles over land. We brought three strings up all told.

In the meantime, we had, of course, gone into the design of the bridge and how we were going to build it. The normal pontoon barge is made up of pontoons which are five feet by seven feet when they're floated in the water and they're five feet deep, but we realized that the five-foot deep section was probably not going to be strong enough - in fact we knew it would not be strong enough - to cantilever across the 80-foot span. So we drew a plan and turned the pontoon up so that it was seven feet high instead of five-feet high, and then by judicious welding of the joints strengthened it and made a structural member out of that seven foot deep by 107 foot long by five foot wide string. And, in order to prove our point and so as to not to become the laughing stock of the whole island - everybody was watching us like a hawk, as you can imagine - we cantilevered this string across the land in what we called

Triest #3 - 113

a dry run, starting with a number of rollers back at the rear end of the string and then, with a tractor, pushing the string across the land to see how far it would go.

On our first attempt, it soon became apparent that we didn't have enough counterbalance, even though the back pontoons at that point had been repaired and filled with water. There was not enough weight on the back part to counteract the weight of the suspended portion, and so we superimposed pontoons on top of the string and filled them with water so as to give the proper counterbalance. Then we completed our dry run operation on the land and as the leading edge of the pontoon got to the 75-foot mark, a tractor with a boom on it - on the forward abutment - was attached to lift the string up just enough to help us with the counterbalancing so that the string could be pushed the entire distance across the span.

At this point we were satisfied that we could launch the string as designed. We then moved the string onto the abutment and placed under the leading edge three sets of rollers which were part of the pontoon gear, then spaced other rollers back on the approaches so that the entire string was supported on the southernmost abutment and approaches. Then we proceeded with our launching operation and the tractor on the southern shore pushed the string across the stream until it got to within three or four feet of the westerly abutment where a tractor on that shore was fastened to the string and raised it a couple of feet so that it could be cleared of the new abutment while the tractor on the far side continued to shove it across. This occupied approximately three hours, I should say.

Following that, we launched the other two strings and did so in fifteen to twenty minutes each. Then came the most difficult part of the problem. These strings which were now sitting in their proper positions, but in the wrong attitudes - in other words, they were in the 7-foot high attitude rather than the 7-foot wide attitude. In the first place, we didn't want just a 15-foot wide bridge, that would not have been wide enough. We wanted a 21-foot wide bridge. The welding that we had done on the strings to make a girder of the pontoons and the structural angles had been designed so that it would give us maximum strength when it was turned on its side representing 5-foot high and 7-foot wide each.

This presented really quite a problem because these pontoon strings were 33 tons each and we only had two tractors, with boom attachments, one on either abutment, and those tractors had to be relied on to lift the pontoons in place and turn them over. Now, lifting that string up and then turning it over presented an inertia problem because we were throwing the weight off center of the cable from the boom of the tractor, and had we not been extremely careful we would have toppled both tractors into the river. So we had to resort to some fancy rigging and positioning of the strings and positioning of the tractors so that we would displace the hoisting cable of each tractor a certain number of feet to the left, we'll say, of the center line of the tractor and when it was hoisted the string came up from a square position to a position where the center line was diagonally across the pontoons, rather than square with the pontoons.

Now we have this box sitting on one edge, so to speak, and then when we slacked off on our cables, the design was such that we would have just that same off center of the cable on the right-hand side as we had on the left-hand side. We were then able to lower the string down onto the abutments again with no strain. It was very easily done and very quietly and we made the placement perfectly. Then we proceeded to do the same thing with the other two strings.

By this time, all of the top brass of the island had collected -

Q: They were all kibitzing!

Capt. T.: They were all kibitzing and they were all very, very skeptical. As a matter of fact, a lot of our boys made bets with the Army and the Marine personnel that were on the island because nobody believed that this could be done. At the end, one of the boys with a very large bet was heard to shout in a loud voice to one of his Marine buddies, "Pay me, sucker."!

Q: This must have been a real morale-builder, to have

undertaken such a difficult engineering feat?

Capt. T.: It was, and I am now reading from the book that we wrote at that time. One of the paragraphs says, "We are like the pioneers. Many of them built bridges, too, but we rehearsed our show and perhaps there we are different. Commander Triest launched the strings first across a road in dress rehearsal before we made any attempt to launch them over the Nalimbu. We knew we couldn't go wrong, that's why we snickered as we covered every bet. It really wasn't fair."

Q: And yet it was, too!

Now, may I ask a question I asked previously? A bridge so constructed with field pontoons was less vulnerable to the river in flood stage and all the debris that came down?

Capt. T.: It was practically invulnerable to the floods, because we had an 80-foot clear span and 80 feet was enough to take any debris that could be washed down and therefore it was washed through the bridge. As a matter of fact, in testimony of that, I heard from a man who'd been out there only two or three years ago, that the bridge was still standing, not so much as a coat of paint had been applied in twenty-four years.

Triest #3 - 117

Q: However, it's still standing in the middle of a jungle, isn't it?

Capt. T.: Probably yes. Incidentally, when we got through and tied the strings together as they would have been in the water as a unit, we then decided to build additional bridges further along the shore. The next pontoon string which we hauled along the shoreline to the next river was stopped in the middle of our bridge and it was calculated that we were applying 45 tons of weight at the center of the span and had less than an inch deflection! Really extraordinary!

Q: Captain, will you answer this question for me? All of these projects were carried on under rather difficult circumstances and with the knowledge that what you did was going to be used only for a very brief period of time. Did this have any influence on your thinking? You were moving on from island to island and you weren't going to be in any one place very long.

Capt. T.: That's true. We were not going to be there, but we knew that the war wasn't over by a long shot and Guadalcanal was going to be used as a supply center and a staging area for future operations. We were a long way from Japan at that point.

I don't think it had much influence on our thinking or on our construction because actually we weren't expending much in the way of material. We were doing it with coral and the amount of steel that we used was minimal, mostly scrap stuff, so that the construction that we were doing was not of an expensive or permanent nature. But it was calculated to last long enough for our purposes.

One interesting episode happened, but I'll come back to that later.

Shortly after this, as I indicated before, we received orders to go to Auckland, for a month's rest and rehabilitation, which, of course, was a tremendous morale-builder. By that time, the boys had finished this bridge job and were doubly in need of a rest, so we embarked for New Zealand.

Q: Was this an escorted troopship?

Capt. T.: No, it was completely unescorted. In fact, there was no danger down in those waters at the time. We were keeping the Japs too busy up north to have them worry about the back waters.

Q: What facilities were there in Auckland for rest and recreation?

Capt. T.: The Red Cross had preceded us there and for a

period of six or eight months had been receiving mostly fliers, I would think, Marine, Army and Navy fliers who had gone down there for rehabilitation, and a few Seabee battalions. They had prepared the way and really done an excellent job. Our experiences in Auckland were quite extraordinary. When we tied up, the Red Cross director and two of his girls came aboard to greet us and the director asked if I would summon the boys on the foredeck and give him a loudspeaker so that he could address us. This was about two o'clock in the afternoon, I guess, or two-thirty, and he told us that we would be going ashore and we would go to a certain camp whose name escapes me at the moment, and that we'd have to unload our gear and get settled in camp before there would be any liberty. This he said, because their experience was that once troops got ashore it was pretty difficult to get any work done. It was physical work as we had about 1,500 tons of gear to move ashore, including a large load of supplies and other things that we'd brought with us.

Then he said, "Now I want to tell you what we have in store for you. We've been here now six or eight months and we've had some rather extensive experience with troops coming down for rest and rehabilitation. I want to prepare you for what it's like, and also to tell you that this is born of our experience with the New Zealanders and our job is to see that we have as little friction as we can and that you have as much fun out of your stay here and make yourselves as welcome as the others have."

"Tonight, for example, we've arranged a dance for you and we'll supply all the dates. But there's one stipulation, that they will come under their own power or under our auspices and we will take them home. There will be no dating after the dance. What you do tomorrow is something else again, but we've promised these girls safe conduct tonight under our auspices. That's the invitation. However, there will be corsages available and you can give them to whomever you choose to honor with a corsage, and we have an excellent orchestra, and so on, and refreshments. The dance is at eight o'clock tonight. So it behooves you to get ashore and cleaned up and have your inspection before you leave camp."

I want to tell you a few more things about conduct. We've found that if we behave ourselves with people we get along very well, but if we allow ourselves to overindulge in almost any way, why, we get into trouble. Obviously, the New Zealand girls are hungry for men. Most of their men have been away for ten years now and their ranks have been depleted horribly in the wars that have preceded this one, so the town is way overpopulated with girls and women. But one thing that I want to emphasize is that we have to date been responsible for very little in the way of venereal disease and I think this is very worthwhile talking about.

Triest #3 - 121

Each of you will be given a physical examination and we will supply you with the necessary protections and we want you to use those protections. All the girls have been - that are on our lists - have been furnished with questionnaires and tomorrow the date bureau will be open at eight thirty in the morning and my Red Cross girls will be there to assist you in getting dates if you haven't got any with somebody coming to the dance tonight. We have about 1,100 girls on our list and the interview cards show first a picture of the girl, her name, her family's name, and what she has been doing, and what her family has been doing, what her father's trade is, the extent of her education, her likes and dislikes, whether she likes history or engineering or whether she likes mechanics, or what-not, plus the vital statistics. And then we asked these girls point blank a very personal question. We asked them whether they will or whether they won't and they've been very frank with us in saying yes, they would if they liked the boy, or no, they wouldn't, and so forth and so on, and we want you to respect that."

Q: Amazingly enlightened, weren't they?

Capt. T.: It was amazing.

"Don't make a date with a girl and expect you're going to get something when she's already said that she's not to be had. Pick somebody that will suit your thinking. Everybody will be happier."

Of course, the shrieks that went up over this just were unbelievable, but the result was that the boys went to the date bureau and they'd give their specifications of the kind of girl they'd like, she'd be tall or short, or fat or slim, or she'd like dancing or she wouldn't like dancing, this, that, and the other thing. Then the Red Cross girl would pointedly say, "Well, now, what about the other? Do you want somebody that will or won't?" The girls were very well schooled and very casual and sincere about it, and the result was there was a minimum of embarrassment and I would say that ninety percent of the dates that were made as a result of this date bureau, this exchange, were girls that the boys stuck with the whole thirty days they were there. Perfectly amazing! Of course, they were privileged to and did leave the camp the next day and stayed with these girls. Some moved into the house with the parents and some moved into apartments with the girls. I suppose we had, maybe, about 200 married men and others that continued to stay in the camp, but the rest of them were off and there were no questions asked. The officers fared very well, too. We were sent to a perfectly magnificent house owned by a Frenchman named Murphy and this house had eight or so bedrooms converted to dormitories and four beds each, or two double beds each, and staffed by Red Cross girls. There were two or three tea dances every

Triest #3 - 123

week and a formal dance every Saturday night, picnics a couple of times a week, the icebox always open with gallons of milk and fresh meat and other things provided, tennis and swimming and so on. The boys really had a perfectly magnificent time.

Of course, New Zealand is really a garden spot. They have in the middle of New Zealand a lake called Rotarua where there is the best trout fishing in the world. It's the home of the famous sportsman, Mr. Cook. The most famous fishing rods in the world at that time were Cook rods. Many of the boys went to Rotarua and would stand at the edge of the lake and cast and bring in a ten or fifteen-pounder without any problem at all. In fact, the record for rainbow trout was 32 pounds, standing on the shoreline and just casting into the lake.

Q: That's also the home of the caverns, isn't it, with the bats?

Capt. T.: I didn't hear anything about that, for some strange reason. I didn't go there myself. My executive officer, Bill Cabaniss, decided, however, that we would go to Mayor Island - Zane Greys famous fishing grounds, on the north of the North Island where the black marlin and mako shark fishing is at its best. Mako sharks run from 800 to 1,100 pounds and the black marlin run from 500 to 800 pounds.

We went there and looked around to find the best boat we

could find and we met a captain who ran regular fishing parties so we went out with him the next day. It was a little bit rough - I wouldn't call it rough, by that I mean we had two or three foot sea state, but it was overcast, and he'd brought along some carwhi which are known in this country as tuna. They were about fifteen or sixteen inches long and he'd put a great big hook in the back of the tuna and cast it overboard and it would swim away hopefully as bait for the bigger fish. We didn't get so much as a strike, not a strike, in that whole day, so we came in pretty discouraged.

The next day, however, two or our pharmacist's mates - I don't suppose that either one weighed more than 110 pounds dripping wet, from Iowa and Illinois went out. Neither of them had ever been on the water before, let alone done any fishing. They went out on a fishing boat with about thirty or thirty-five others and each one of them caught a fish. One of them was a 550-pound striped marlin and the other was a 700-pound black marlin. So that was, of course, the highlight of their trip, fantastic.

On the way home we went to Russell Island, which is off the eastern coast, and there the principal fishing was for striped marlin and they run from about 400 to about 650 pounds. We again got a boat and noticed that the captain didn't have any bait. "Oh," he said, "don't worry about that. We'll get plenty of bait on the way out." So, on the way out, he suddenly swerved the boat about 45 degrees to the right and we could see ahead of us about two miles a gigantic light spot in the water, absolutely gigantic, and he explained that there were probably half a million to a million tuna in that school.

We went right to the school and then he said, "Now, if you'll just stand one on either side at the stern and just drop your bare hooks in, you'll catch all the tuna you can use." We no sooner hit the school than the reverberation of the tails of these fish on the bottom of the hull was like a staccato. You couldn't hear yourself talk or think. All we could do was drop our hooks and pull the fish in. I think when it came to crossing that school, which was probably about 3/4 of a mile in diameter, we took in about thirty-seven fish to use as bait. Having passed the school, we went to the left again out to the fishing grounds for the larger fish. Once again we didn't even have a nibble. Neither one of us was a fisherman so it wasn't surprising, but it was a great disappointment because here we were in the greatest fishing grounds in the world and not to catch a single fish!

Q: You had the wrong bait!

Capt. T.: Well, that was a great month and the boys got an enormous amount out of it. Incidentally, I think we left about 500 babies behind -

Triest #3 - 126

Q: I was going to ask that question!

Capt. T.: Very, very welcome to the New Zealanders. Their attitude about it was very much the same as the attitude of the Swedes. They take care of unwed mothers and I don't think that any one of our boys was ever questioned, harangued, harassed, or asked to marry any of the girls after they left the islands.

Q: Were there a number of marriages?

Capt. T.: None that I know of. There may have been, but I don't think there were any marriages on the island. That was one of the things that we cautioned the boys about. After all, they were in a strange land and while a girl may look awfully sweet to him here, his first thought must be to think of her transported back to his own native locale and would she fit into his own milieu at home?

Q: How many men were there involved in this period of rest?

Capt. T.: In this movement we had a full complement. We had about 1,100 officers and men. Anyway, we finished that tour very happily and returned to Guadalcanal and found our camp pretty much of a wreck due to a recent storm. So we spent considerable time rebuilding it and getting organized and carrying on some further construction work before getting ready to move forward.

Our next move then was to Emirau.

Q: How long a period of time before you moved on to Emirau?

Capt. T.: I think about two weeks. Not more than three. Then, as I say, we moved to Emirau, which was northwest of Guadalcanal, perhaps about 300 miles. On the move to Emirau, we didn't know - and why, I don't know - that the island was not occupied.

Q: You mean that there were no natives on it?

Capt. T.: No natives, no Japanese, but we thought there were. It was a pretty rugged coast and it would have been impossible to land without some land aid force, particularly the equipment, without some preparation. So 45 of us including two officers embarked with the Marines - and I think there were maybe a thousand Marines - and/the first landing on the first day. We brought with us a couple of tractors with bulldozer attachments, and were accompanied by and were actually under the command of a Captain Bill Painter, whose name you may recall, a famous civil engineer and another chap whose name escapes me for the moment. Painter had been responsible for the initial surveying of a great many of the islands throughout the Pacific prior to any landings. He would go ashore in

Triest #3 - 128

PT boats and also by plane would do a lot of observation work. He would decide that this was a suitable place to land and so on, and with air photography was able to prepare the way for a great many of our landings and also the preparation of harbors. For example, the coral had to be blasted out - to make channels for landing craft. This was easily observed through aerial photography. When he went ashore he and another man are reported to have traversed more than a hundred miles of the Chinese coast looking the situation over and finding out where the best eventual landing places might be -

Q: In China?

Capt. T.: In China - if we should have to go there. Oddly enough, with this great war career that he had, he returned and was out one day with his wife in his boat on the Potomac and there was a backfire and he was killed.

Q: Why was this particular island selected?

Capt. T.: Topographically it was selected because it looked to be the flattest from the point of view of quick preparation for aircraft. In other words, the building of an airfield for fighter planes. Actually, we set off on the second day with Painter and four or five surveyors and began surveying the site of the fighter strip that we built on Emirau, even while we were preparing for the landing of the main body of troops. In that preparation we bulldozed down a large section of a cliff and pushed the coral out into the water to afford a beach for landing craft and discharge of cargo. The natural beach was so flat that we couldn't have gotten in within three or four hundred yards with a boat of any draft.

Q: Some of the surrounding islands were occupied by the Japanese, were they not?

Capt. T.: Ah, yes. Truk was one of the important islands that was -

Q: This was not far from Truk?

Capt. T.: No, it was only about thirty or forty miles from Truk.

The main body of troops with the Army came ashore the next day and we started immediately building the airfield. I don't remember how long it took us, but I think in sixty-six days we had the field in operation.

Q: What about the other facilities?

Capt. T.: Well, we were at the same time building landing facilities for cargo ships, port facilities, a hospital, various camps, entertainment facilities, and theaters. We built General Boyd's headquarters, chapel, et cetera.

Q: General Boyd being the island commander?

Capt. T.: The Army island commander.

Q: So this was a total project, and it was the first one you were involved in, wasn't it?

Capt. T.: It was the first one that I was involved in on my own, yes. After we'd been there a couple of months, the USO troops began coming in. One of the first entertainment groups was Jack Benny and a couple of others. They entertained us royally. He was followed by Bob Hope and a girl named Patty Thomas. However, this was an experience which I won't put on tape - suffice to say that the whole affair was disgusting.

Q: You were disgusted with it?

Capt. T.: I was totally disgusted with Hope's attitude and his unspeakable show, but it was one of those things which would have been a political death knell had General Boyd reported it, so we kept quiet and let it go at that.

Q: How long did it take you to accomplish all these various

construction jobs on this particular island?

Capt. T.: I think we were pretty well completed in about three months.

Q: That was rather remarkable! How many men did you hope to accommodate on the island?

Capt. T.: We didn't build shore facilities for more than a thousand mostly Marine fighters, and there were no other troops - well, there was one battalion of Army on the other end of the island - but the principal purpose of the island was as a fighter base for the Marines.

Q: What about the floating dry docks? What sort of repair facilities were envisioned?

Capt. T.: We had no repair facilities and no dry docks at Emirau. The last dry docks that had been built were pontoon dry docks that we used in Tulagi. But nothing farther north, as far as I know.

Q: This was a heavily jungled island, too, wasn't it?

Capt. T.: Very heavy jungle and the banyon trees, of course, were the bane of our existence. We had a terrible time trying to remove them.

The bulk of our pontoon experience was in building pontoon dry docks in Tulagi. On the right-hand side of the particular picture I'm showing you now, is the principal island of Tulagi. The pontoons were being built across the bay at a point called Halava. The handling of the pontoon construction was quite extensive, as you can see here. We had a platform about ten pontoons wide with pontoons erected vertically on each side. When the main strings of pontoons were filled with water, the dry dock sank. They were, however, each individually compartmented so they could be de-watered and were used to raise ships for repair purposes.

Q: Captain, you said that on Emirau Island there were no natives whatsoever. I know there were on some of the other islands you worked on. Would you, as a kind of a footnote, say a few words about the native population that you did encounter, their attitudes, their sense of cooperation, or lack of cooperation?

Capt. T.: The only natives that I encountered were the natives on Espiritu Santo and Guadalcanal. They were principally pretty pathetic people. In other words, their health was not good and certainly they were not of any stature. They were very weak, emaciated kind of people, by and large. There were no natives on Emirau. There wasn't a living soul on Emirau, much to our surprise, as I've indicated.

Q: Was there any effective cooperation, or was this necessary?

Capt. T.: There was tremendous cooperation with the natives. As a matter of fact - I'm not sure now whether this occurred while we were at Tulagi or while we were still at Guadalcanal, but one of our boys invented a giant "can opener". It was nothing more than what we now know as a beer-can opener only it had a telescopic handle and when it opened up it was about 14 inches long, as opposed to seven inches long in a closed position. We picked eight or ten of the best natives that we could get and used to send them forward with PT boats to Green Island and one or two other islands. They were put ashore at night with these can openers, and on one particular occasion we believed that they destroyed something in excess of 4,000 fifty-five gallon drums of gasoline by just puncturing a hole in the bottom and the top of each of these drums which they found in small caches that the Japs had spread around judiciously because they wanted to avoid large concentration of fuel against our bombing attacks. So they would stash twenty-five here and twenty-five there and our boys went around very quietly during the night and punctured them letting the gasoline waste away.

We think we did a lot to shorten the war in that area as

Can opener - used by friendly natives put ashore on Jap held islands to destroy some 4,000 55 gallon drums of gasoline.

a result of those forays.

Q: And the natives were cooperative?

Capt. T.: The natives did it, our boys didn't do it. One of the things that was interesting was in connection with the man who developed this can opener. I sent a secret dispatch through recommending that he be awarded a medal and never heard one peep out of it, never got any acknowledgment. I couldn't get any awards for any of our boys. I may have gotten a couple of Purple Hearts and a couple of Bronze Stars and there were one or two other medals given to the boys for particularly meritorious things, but, generally speaking, we had nothing, no recognition for the work that our boys did - not even a battalion citation.

Q: Was this ever reported to some of the senior officers who were concerned about adequate recognition?

Capt. T.: No. Frankly, we were busy and we didn't know at that time that this wasn't the standard procedure. But it developed that in every case we were reporting under the Army command. They were busy with their own people and not concerned with what the Seabees did.

Q: You were not within the Navy chain of command?

Capt. T.: No. The Island Command was Army.

Q: Were you ever in touch with some of the, I guess you'd call them coast watchers, the Australians who were on some of these islands and were reporting Jap ship movements?

Capt. T.: I never personally encountered any of them. I know that we had our own intelligence people, not the Seabees but the Navy had its own people along the shores, but I don't recall ever meeting any of the Australians or New Zealanders.

Q: When you were on an island like Emirau the Japanese must have been cognizant of the fact that you were there and building a base. Were you subjected to raids at night?

Capt. T.: We had our friend Washing Machine Charlie, a Jap observer, but again what he saw wasn't followed up by any bombing strikes because our Navy was keeping them too busy at forward bases to worry about what was happening down the line.

Q: But in this case you were only forty miles from Truk?

Capt. T.: Yes, but at that point Truk had been fairly well neutralized and whatever bombing the Japs were doing was concentrated more on our shipping lanes and large accumulations of ships rather than on an individual isolated island.

I said earlier that we didn't use much cement in our construction operations, and the reason for that was that the cement that they sent out to us, coming in Stateside bags as it did and having been subjected to very high humidity, the bags had not only become saturated, we couldn't adequately cover them up, but they had been torn and therefore the cement –

Q: Was already concrete!

Capt. T.: That's right, and it wasn't worth anything. We decided, however, that since we had about 10,000 bags that we had brought ashore, we would reconstitute it. We put in a crusher and established a conveyor system and proceeded to salvage the cement and put it in fifty-five gallon drums. I think when we got through with it, only about thirty percent was usable.

Q: As a result of that experience, did a recommendation go back that future shipments should be in drums?

Capt. T.: It most certainly did. Whether they ever did it or not, I don't know, but we certainly tried.

Q: Would you say a word at this point about the flow of supplies, the raw materials needed for your various construction projects? Was there improvement in the flow?

Capt. T.: Oh, yes, as we went along there was immense improvement. You see, we'd been back to the States for six months - no, I beg your pardon, we hadn't been back as yet, but the improvement had already started to become felt through new shipments of stuff that were coming forward. In other words, they had changed their supply lists from something that was quite ungainly in the beginning to much more utilitarian type of list as each operation developed to indicate that we needed more of this and less of that. Also, that cement was not, for example, a prime requisite building material for the island type of operation for we could get three-quarters of the work done with coral judiciously used. Prior to our experience in the island the Navy didn't realize that coral was an excellent building material, and they thought they'd have to supply cement for all purposes.

That's how we happened to have 10,000 bags of cement on Emirau. We didn't need a bag of it, actually.

Q: The utilization of coral was a lesson well learned. It must have been a known asset in various parts of the world, I would think, in the Caribbean.

Capt. T.: It probably was and I think it should have been as far as we were concerned, but you see in normal civilian life coral is not sufficiently stable to build anything except roads. In the Caribbean they've always build roads out of coral, but they never use coral for any other building purposes, even military operations. But when we got there we found that there was no sense in building a concrete structure if you do not have reinforcing rods and we had no reinforcing. We only had coral to use as a sand cement ingredient. Without reinforcing roads concrete is only about one-tenth as strong as it would be if reinforced.

Q: It lacked its backbone!

Capt. T.: That's right.

Q: Were there similar lessons that you learned in the South Pacific comparable to the one about using coral? Were there other structural lessons that you learned as an engineer?

Capt. T.: Well, I think that the use of the pontoons in bridge construction was the principal lesson that we learned. In other words, using pontoons like the building blocks that they were was a very, very valuable lesson. No civilian engineer would have thought that they could put the pontoons to use that way, to the multiple uses that we did, such as the building of landing facilities. We used pontoons extensively on top of coral causeways to form a bulkhead against which ships could land ten feet high - in ten feet of water. We'd fill the pontoons with sand and tie them together on two sides of a causeway, and then fill up the middle of the causeway with coral. We thus made causeways 25, or 30, or 40 feet wide with a bulkhead of pontoons along each side. This, again, was a use for which the pontoons hadn't been conceived.

Q: Was there anything in the area of dealing with the torrential rains and constant downpours, the tropical situation - anything that was valuable that you might have learned through that experience? You had to go on.

Capt. T.: Nothing that I can specifically point to, except possibly the malarial control that we instituted that was quite extensive. In other words, drainage and an effective way to eliminate stagnant ponds and pools of water, and then the judicious application of a fuel oil to the surface of ponds to kill the malaria mosquito.

Q: This soon assumed a great importance. I mean the preliminary steps.

Capt. T.: We couldn't have carried on the war if we hadn't been able to eradicate malaria. Malaria was in profusion. Everybody had malaria. Everybody was taking atabrin or quinine twice a day and so on.

Q: Atabrin was a new drug, wasn't it?

Capt. T.: It was a new drug at that point, and then they brought out another one. I've forgotten its name now, but it got to be in quite short supply because everybody had to have it. As I say, if it hadn't been for DDT and the fuel oil that we were able to spread on top of some of these swampy areas, we just couldn't have carried on. One thing that we were not able effectively to combat was jungle rot, perfectly horrible skin infection which was not only a peeling skin but it developed severe rashes and red sores and itch.

Q: Almost like leprosy!

Capt. T.: Almost, and it itched so that it just drove you out of your mind.

Q: Was that a lack of citric acid?

Capt. T.: No, we called it jungle rot. We had oranges to combat scurvy from the States. This was just plain jungle rot. In other words, everything was soaking wet all the time, all the time, all the time. It rained, rained, rained and with the heat and the humidity, I suppose only one out of twenty men escaped breaking out in this horrendous rash.

Q: Were the native people subject to this as well, or were they immune?

Capt. T.: I really don't know. Those that we saw for the most part were pretty pitiful sights and covered with sores one way or another, and bothered by thousands of flies. Whether that was disease - there was a lot of elephantiasis, for example. We found one poor fellow that had to carry his genitals around in a wheelbarrow, he was that far gone.

Q: Some of our men were afflicted, too, weren't they?

Capt. T.: Yes, they were but not, of course, to such an extent. But these natives were afflicted with perfectly astounding diseases.

Q: Was there any cure for that?

Capt. T.: At that time, I don't think so, but they've learned a lot since. I've heard of a few of our people that contracted it but when they were sent Stateside they improved and were cured.

Q: Because of the nature of the disease, was there not any fear among our men of being afflicted?

Triest #3 - 142

Capt. T.: I don't think so, no, because in the first place our men were pretty decently fed and the sanitation conditions under which we lived were such as to fairly well preclude that we were going to get into that kind of a problem.

Q: Going back to the engineering lessons you learned, in retrospect as you came back into civilian life and as you continue your profession, have you seen any carryover of lessons from that period in that part of the world to what you do nowadays?

Capt. T.: I think the most notable one I've already recounted - the IBM cards. We think fondly that we were the forerunner of the present IBM system. I still have to get the exact period when we developed the cards.

Q: But as for engineering techniques, you don't think of anything that really has proved advantageous?

Capt. T.: I don't think so because we were really doing only the most elementary things. Nothing really that hadn't been done for centuries before only with better requipment -

Q: It seems to me you were pretty innovative in some of the things that you did, the bridge-building.

Capt. T.: That's true, we were, but we had to make do. Like making, for instance, our own hot-water heaters out of oil drums. In other words, we made oil burners to make hot-water heaters to sanitize our mess kits, whereas the rest of the forces just built a fire under a can and heated water that way but we would turn on a burner and make boiling water with steam in very short order. When we got through we turned it off. We made showers that way, hot-water showers.

As I look at the book, for instance, I'm looking at what we called Duffy's torture machine, which was an orthopedic table designed for one of the hospitals. As you will notice, the bottom half of this table, where the man is lying can be rotated from side to side.

Q: To exercise his vertebrae!

Capt. T.: For treatment purposes. On the opposite page is a picture of component parts of a lathe which our boys made out of odd bits and pieces because we had to have some machine-turning equipment and this lathe particularly was used in connection with our ship-repair work.

Q: You must have encouraged a flock of inventors as a result of this!

Capt. T.: One of the things that we did while we were on Emirau and had finished our principal work and in order to get ready for future assignments was to build a very modern rifle range. We required everybody to go through a marksmanship course and, of course, a great many of the boys won marksmanship medals as a result of this. This was a good morale-builder and it was a very scientifically controlled series of targets.

Q: Was this an overall requisite for Seabees, or was it peculiar to your own units?

Capt. T.: We did it ourselves because at that time we were getting a little desperate as to what to do next and this was good therapy.

We had another morale-builder. We built some very attractive chapels and the chapel on Emirau was no exception. This was done with odd bits of wood and so on. You see here that the lights in the ceiling were all a modern type of lighting fixture. We even had simulated organ pipes at the end of the chancel and we used our portable organ that we had taken with us. The organ pipes in the background gave it reality, and then with the stained-glass window -

Q: How did you make stained-glass windows?

Capt. T.: With paint on glass, various shades of paint, and put them together with strips - I don't know whether we used actual pieces of lead or what the joints were composed of, but for all the world you'd think it was a stained-glass window.

Q: And here, in the case of the chapel, you tried to maintain a traditional place of worship?

Capt. T.: We did, indeed.

Q: And this for obvious reasons. Tell me about the role of the chaplain with the Seabees?

Capt. T.: The chaplain, of course, was a very important part of our whole complement. As I explained earlier, when I got to Tulagi I found that they had shipped a Catholic chaplain out with the battalion. He was rather lacking in sense of humor and had very little tolerance. As a result he had not given the boys any comfort, and so it was decided that he ought to be replaced as soon as we could do so, and he was. We got a young fellow named Lieutenant Anderson who was a perfectly remarkable chaplain, Episcopal, and he was at the same time recreation officer. One of the things that he instituted was soft ball, the building of a soft ball team. This team performed quite notably and won the championship of the island over teams from several other units. One of the boys had been killed in one of the raids, a chap named Mansfield, and we built a playing field and bleachers and called it Mansfield Stadium. At that time there was a great push on to sell war bonds, so what we did was to conserve our beer supply and our beef until we had one of these games. Then we built what we called Andy's Hamburger Stand - this came later, but at Andy's Hamburger Stand we would allow a man to buy a case of beer at a time - or rather, we'd give him a case of beer for every $500 bond he bought, and half a case of beer for every $250 bond.

Q: These would be deductions from his pay? Or did he have to fork up the cash?

Capt. T.: He had to fork up the cash, and most of them had it in their hands. You've never seen so much cash in your life. While most of the boys had allotments they had no place else to spend their extra money and with a little judicious poker-playing and crap shooting, they accumulated lots of money, so it was not very difficult to sell hamburgers for 25 cents for the welfare fund -

Q: Wasn't that a fairly stiff price for a hamburger in those days?

Capt. T.: Yes, but we made excellent hamburger rolls. You'd think you were at any Stateside hamburger joint, and we made pickles and other things, and served beer and soft drinks. These games were really quite an experience. We used to have audiences of anywhere from 1,500 to 2,000 men. This was a morale duty or facet of the chaplain's position, actually, if you wish to call it that, and indicated his extreme importance to us. I know that he was particularly influential in assuaging the homesickness of a lot of these boys.

Q: The pastoral aspect!

Capt. T.: Yes.

Q: And what about the chapel services themselves? I mean how frequent were they?

Capt. T.: We had chapel service every Sunday morning and, as I say, we had a portable organ which we usually found somebody to play and we sang hymns and so on, and conducted a regular service. It was very inspiring. This chaplain was a tremendous fellow.

Q: What about the celebration of the Mass for the Roman Catholics?

Capt. T.: We had a Roman Catholic service for them and we had a Jewish service for the Jewish boys, and we had communion services.

Q: All performed by the same chaplain?

Capt. T.: No. He doubled with other battalions where they didn't have an Episcopal chaplain and the others came over to us.

Q: Oh, I see.

As you describe some of these things that were accomplished in the recreational field and what have you. Did you sometimes sit back and reflect and be utterly amazed at what a group of men could accomplish under difficult circumstances?

Capt. T.: It was a source of constant amazement and something quite unexpected because in civilian life, of course, in this country a man works eight hours, or did in those days - now he's working five - but in those days they put in a good eight hours' work. I myself had been used to working ten hours a day in my subway building building experience. But overseas, when we got through we had chow and then we had many, many more hours of either boredom or a chance to do something worthwhile. We found that nine-tenths of the boys, except when there was a movie on, turned to something profitable to do, largely as an escape from boredom, of course but also because they were impelled to do something for progressive and morale reasons. The manning of the antiaircraft batteries, for example, and the forays in the PT boats were all part of this same scheme. The boys were anxious to do something, get the war over with, and we found that more square pegs could be put into round holes than you could shake a stick at. You wouldn't believe, in other words, that a man could be a carpenter in the daytime, could be a moving picture operator at night, and could sing in the choir the next day, could man an antiaircraft gun on occasion during the week, could come out and help with the salvage of a boat, and so on.

It was a constant source of amazement at the latent talents that these boys had. I'm sure it's the same thing today, but they're not given the opportunity and they don't seek the opportunity. They go home at night and they may fuss around the garden a little bit or with a boat, but I don't think any of us is using our talents to one-tenth, of the degree that we could use them if guided and given the proper incentive.

Q: Pursuing that and quite apart from the Seabees, but pursuing that thought today, we are a whole generation of people who do not exercise these very talents, and do they not atrophy after a while, potential atrophy?

Capt. T.: Will you state that again?

Q: Given a set of circumstances similar to the one that we've been talking about in the South Pacific today, with a group of men of our time who have, for most of their lives and perhaps entire lives, not had an opportunity or not taken an opportunity to exercise the various potential talents they have, do you think today they would be able to perform in the same manner that the men you talk about in the South Pacific performed?

Capt. T.: I don't think there's any question in the world about it.

Q: Potential doesn't vanish?

Capt. T.: I don't think it vanishes. I think it improves with age and with experience and from generation to generation. In other words, everybody, at least theoretically, is influenced by what his ancestors have done. He's also inspired by what his peers are doing today, and by the same token, as we progress through life I think we find that one invention leads to the development of another and another, and the more inventions that come along, the faster we progress.

For example, take the development of electronics in World War II. We have progressed in the development of electronics and electronic gear, notably computers, for example, at a fantastic rate since World War II largely because it was a new field that required development. I'm thinking now of space requirements. I think boys and girls today are doing more than we could reasonably have expected them to do twenty or twenty-five years ago. You see kids that are computer operators today getting $25,000 a year and they're 25 years old. You wonder where they could have accumulated all that knowledge in such a short period of time. I think it is latent ability because of their forefathers' experiences which are coming to the fore now. I think that our whole way of life is geared that way, wherever it is given a chance to nurture itself. On the other hand, I think that our whole population has deteriorated immeasurably in the last twenty-five years, that we've just gone to pot as a whole. In other words, I think a certain small segment of our people have gone uphill, whereas a large segment of our people are going downhill in morals and in spirit and in ambition.

Q: But you maintain that the segment that's gone downhill is capable of doing much more under different circumstances?

Capt. T.: That's right.

Q: Very encouraging!

Capt. T.: It is encouraging. Of course, I'm an eternal optimist, but that's the way I feel about it. I think we've got a tremendous potential and some are taking advantage of it and others, unfortunately, have just gone downhill.

As we were finishing our tour on Emirau, scuttlebutt had been flying back and forth very freely and finally when orders came to go home and to embark in a certain ship, I called the battalion together. I had prepared in advance three cards,

14 by 14 cards, and I had printed "Y" on one and "E" on another and "S" on another and I held these behind me as I faced the battalion. Instead of saying anything I held up the cards in order Y-E-S. They all knew exactly what was happening. We were going home! The scuttlebutt was true!

Q: Visual aids!

Capt. T.: There's a very interesting little poem that was written by one of our boys entitled "Scuttlebutt" that I would like to read:

>What's the latest scuttlebutt
>That starts at break of dawn?
>Long before we quit our sack
>What's new? Buddies yawn.
>Someone said we're leaving soon.
>How soon, did they say?
>Oh, about the 1st of June.
>Hell, I heard in May.
>What's the latest scuttlebutt,
>Someone asked at chow?
>Hitler wants to end the war,
>Wants to quit it now.
>Turkeys troops are in the field
>Yeah, that's what I hear.
>Wonder what the Japs will do

With our fleet all here.

What's the latest scuttlebutt?

Never what's the news.

Rumor sweeps from tent to tent

Growing as it moves.

A sack of mail came in today,

Heard that there were ten.

Heard so many bags arrived

Had to build a tent.

There will be no chow tonight,

All the cooks are ill.

Someone saw a Jap last night

Signal through the hills.

Half battalion's going home

This made 'em nuts.

Sharks bit through a PT boat,

Say the scuttlebutts.

What's the latest scuttlebutt?

What the hell do'you know?

When you think we're going home?

When d'you think we'll go?

Even should we meet our fate

And our lips be shut

Some will lag with deadened limbs

What's the scuttlebutt?

That's written by a chap named Alfred Hart.

Q: Captain, we talked about the men and how they occupied themselves in off-hours, what was done for their entertainment. You've given me very little clue as to what you were able to accomplish in terms of relaxation after a long day of commanding these men on the various projects.

Capt. T.: Well, I was fortunate in that I'm a bridge player and a poker player and inevitably we found among our own officers, but most among officers of my own rank in other outfits, excellent bridge games. So after a hard day in the time available the most enjoyable thing was a game of bridge. A number of the boys did the same thing, but of course their particular recreation was the crap table which one of our boys built, looking pretty professional at that. Where he got the green baize, I don't know, but he covered his table with green baize. Some said that he'd been a professional gambler in civilian life. Of course, he had more money than anybody else in the battalion but it was always a source of satisfaction to the enlisted men to participate in those games.

We had movies every night, some were good and some were bad, but for the most part we were able, again through the chaplain, to arrange for exchange of movies with ships and with other island facilities films that came in by aircraft. We did a little swimming, not very much, to be sure, because the coral reefs were awfully sharp on your feet. You had to be particularly careful not to cut yourself because a coral infection can be quite severe, particularly out there when you're already faced with jungle rot. This would just be an opener and could lead to very serious infection.

Interview #4 with Captain Willard G. Triest

Place: Annapolis, Maryland

Date: August 19, 1972

Subject: Biography

By: John T. Mason, Jr.

Mr. Mason: It's nice to see you today, Sir. This chapter is to be concerned with your trip back home to the States after completing your job on the island of Emirau. When you concluded last time, you had just informed your men that the battalion was to be returned to the United States for rest and relaxation.

Captain Triest: Yes, we were sorely in need of it at that point. The spirits, however, were excellent. We had done a good job and recovered from the earlier malaise that had hampered the battalion's efforts during its last year on Tulagi.

Mr. Mason: This seemed to have been a complete recovery?

Captain Triest: It was a complete recovery, indeed it was.

Mr. Mason: Did you get commended for this effort?

Captain Triest: Very much so. There were several letters of commendation to the battalion, but I really feel that there was too little appreciation in the form of decorations for the men themselves possibly because I didn't push hard enough. Most awards, as you know, are pushed by somebody. In the case of the naval units on the islands in the Pacific, they were for the most part under Army command.

Q: And you were not an old line Navy man, so you wouldn't necessarily know that this was the way it was done.

Capt. T.: I had no knowledge of it, actually.

I subsequently found out that the way medals are awarded is that the commanding or division officer puts the bee in some friend's bonnet and he said, "All right, write up a commendation and I'll endorse it," and so on. But we were actually too busy - 12 to 14 hours a day seven days a week - doing the job to think about that sort of thing.

Mr. Mason: There were thousands of men who didn't get recognition in the Navy.

Capt. T.: No question about it. One clear example was the case of the "Can Opener". I actually didn't spend a whole lot of time or effort to bring this case to fruition and unfortunately the powers that were again didn't even realize the value of that development or chose not to pay attention to it. Actually, before leaving Tulagi I was awarded a bronze star for the work that we had done, as was the case also of one of the other unit commanders - not a Seabee, but one of the unit commanders - in a very nice ceremony that General Boyd had for us. And also one of my men received a bronze star for a spectacular job that he had done. That's as far as it went; we didn't even get a unit citation, much as we merited it not only for the tremendous ship repair jobs we performed - 450 all told, including changing 150 props under water - while we were on Tulagi.

After the word was received that we were going home, I had my meeting with the men, and shortly thereafter we embarked. Our route was to take us to Guadalcanal and directly back to the States.

Q: With no further work to perform?

Capt. T.: No further work. We went back, however, on one of the slow Liberty ships. It was originally scheduled to take something in excess of four weeks, but it developed that we were more than five weeks en route because when we stopped at Guadalcanal, of all the ridiculous things we were detained loading 10,000 cases of empty Coke bottles. I almost had a **mutiny** on my hands. Once more the frightful inefficiency of war.

Q: This was an effort on the part of the government to get

the refund value . . .

Capt. T.: The refund value, and I resume the glass shortage was an important factor. This was, of course, before we had aluminum or other containers. I'm sure the Coca Cola companies were screaming for the empties to be returned, but the two were way out of balance.

The value of the ship lying idle for almost a week while these bottles were loaded aboard was just frightful. We had the devil's own time trying to deep the boys busy - there was nothing they could do. They couldn't go ashore, they had no liberty. They just sat there for five days while we took on this cargo. It just made everybody furious. We had to counter by having enforced setting up exercises on the deck and stringent daily inspection of quarters and of personnel and so on - just to give the boys something else to complain about.

I was able to implement something which I had vaguely thought about but again it only came to fruition as a result of necessity engendered by our extended period at sea. That was the putting together of a story of the accomplishments of the battalion during the last three years they had been in the South Pacific.

Q: A very laudable idea. Were you history oriented?

Capt. T.: Not in the slightest, but I was prompted, as I say,

Triest #4 - 160

to generate something for the boys to do. I hit on the idea as being something quite different and apart from what they had been doing, or from what I had been doing, yet I could see this was going to be a considerable time consumer.

Q: I suspect there's an element of pride in what your men had accomplished, too.

Capt. T.: Very much so, but as I was not a part of it, I was able to get their story together from a third party point of view. It was really much more gratifying than if I had written it as part of the whole scene. I was in command only during their last eight months in the South Pacific, but they had had almost two years prior to my joining them during which time they had done some excellent work.

I had a meeting with the officers and outlined my proposition and asked for volunteers to help with the major elements of getting this book together. Initially, of course, we had to outline the proposition to the boys and ask their cooperation in submitting stories and so on which I was going to take . . .

Q: How did they respond to this?

Capt. T.: There was a lot of discussion immediately of course, even during our meeting - a lot of excitement was generated - the anticipation of seeing their names in print and telling their stories. This was fine.

I had this meeting and outlined it all and named the officers who were going to take part in the collation of the stories and the interviews that were going to be conducted, et cetera.

To retrace my steps a little bit now - we had the meeting and I said that I felt that the battalion had done such a remarkable job while they had been in the South Pacific that this story ought to be captured on paper and printed. I was going to make every effort to have the story written and published by a responsible publisher if it was at all possible. I would, therefore, ask each man to write a story or a dozen stories about his experiences in the Pacific detailing where he was and who his friends were and what they had done and so on - giving impressions of the type of job that was required of us. I think we asked for these stories in two or three days, and they began coming in almost immediately, all of them of course written by hand.

You've never seen such a conglomeration of writing in your whole life - some of them written on tablet forms, some of them written on the backs of envelopes, the tensing of course was out of this world. Only in a very few cases did they give the last names of the boys they referred to - Jake and Snake and Tom and Mulberry - without giving any indication who the people were, nor did they say where these stories originated from, what area, or what date or even time. The boys for the most part were not more than high school graduates, and they were construction workers. The more advanced of course were carpenters, mechanics, steel workers, electricians, et cetera, but they were about a five percent compared with the truck drivers, bulldozer operators, the concrete workers and so on.

When these stories started coming in it looked like the most horrendous job that anybody had ever tackled. As I said, they didn't tell you where they were, whether it was night or day, they didn't tell you who they were talking about, or what company they belonged to, or what the assignment was.

Q: Did the author attach his name to his story?

Capt. T.: Oh yes, he'd sigh it Joe S. or in some cases Joe Smith, but that was as far as we got.

Then it became the job of each company commander through his chiefs to locate the man who had written a particular story. The chief and company commander or company officer - each company had four officers - would sit down with this fellow and try to add to his story and get the information, such as his full name and rank, and where they were, and chronologically when it was, what they did, and what the specific job of that particular unit was. In other words - were they building a compass rose or were they erecting a tank farm or were they concerned with ship repair, and if so, what kind. Were they replacing a propeller on a boat, or working on a drive shaft or whatnot.

So attached to each of these original stories then was the supplementary information that the officers were able to obtain.

Q: May I ask what facilities you had on board the Liberty ship for implementing this?

Capt. T.: I think we had at least six typewriters fortunately and yeoman who could handle the work.

We realized the first thing that had to be done was that each piece of paper had to be written double spaced on a typewriter. On fifty percent of them you probably couldn't read the writing. The yeomen's job first was to write the thing out as it was written in double or triple space, so that we at least could read the words. The spelling was corrected as much as possible in that first re-writing.

The next job was to tense each story for as you read each piece you were so constantly upset with the tensing - that you had great difficulty getting any reasoning out of the story. That was the second re-writing.

Then the third re-writing was to crank into these stories the essentials of place, time, names, locations, et cetera.

It then became a question of collating all the stories so that we could put them in some kind of chronological order - the work that we had actually done on Tulagi, at Guadalcanal, and finally at Emirau, plus a months rest in New Zealand.

Triest #4 - 164

Q: Some of those things you couldn't talk about . . .

Capt. T.: That's right. We were quite frank about it - about our impact on New Zealand. I don't know whether I mentioned specifically - our estimate was that we had left about five hundred babies behind in Auckland, which I'm sure has been a very worthwhile contribution to their civilization and the cross-breeding of national stocks. You see, they had been at war for seven years before we came and the country's manpower had been terribly depleted. Nationally they welcomed the prospect of an increased birth rate and actually subsidized expectant mothers.

But to continue, we somehow, largely with the aid of our bookwriting experiences, were able to suffer through the forty-five days necessary to get us back to San Francisco.

Q: Did you have anybody on your staff who had experience with editorship?

Capt. T.: No one. I had one officer, though, who had been an English teacher, and one officer who had studied a little history. But for the most part I had nobody that had ever had any editing or writing experience.

When we arrived in San Francisco we were sent to Camp Parks which was the large rehabilitation center in the valley just east of the city. We were released for leave and I think within a matter of two days everybody had gone about their separate business.

When we reconvened we were told we then had at least six weeks before we might be shipped out again. That was the time when we finally decided that we'd have to have a professional writer put all the material that we had developed into readable form. So we engaged a gentleman who was a former writer on the Chicago TRIBUNE - he was free lancing - whose name at the moment escapes me. Out of our welfare funds we engaged him for I think $1500 to come to Camp Parks and talk to us about the book and re-write it and get it in shape for printing. The first thing he wanted to do - which was a surprise to me at the beginning, but of course I immediately saw the reasoning - was talk to all the boys and personally quiz them about the stories that they had written. We thought we had done it, but of course we didn't do it from a writer's point of view. So these boys had to go through it all again. He spent from a half to three-quarters of an hour with every boy who had contributed discussing his particular stories. Of course a lot of them he didn't bother with as they weren't sufficiently important.

Q: I hope you'll tell me also about the assembling of the excellent photographs that ultimately found their way into "Meat On The Table."

Capt. T.: This of course went along with our repetition of

the stories to him and his examination of our pictures. We had an official photographer with us as did every battalion. So these pictures were all available, and he used them to illustrate our story.

Every one of the pictures in the book depicted something of importance, whether it was the erection of a floating drydock for example, or the building of an assembly line whereby we re-claimed a great portion of 10,000 bags of cement.

Our writer finished his story and gave me the manuscript which we proceeded to correct for about the tenth time. Then I took the work to Doubleday-Doran. One of the vice-presidents was a great friend of mine, but he regretfully had to tell me that he couldn't print it because they had just published a book about the Seabees.

This had been generated within the Civil Engineer Corps by a man named Huey, whom we nicknamed "Hooey" because everything that he wrote was so much hooey as far as we were concerned. And I say that for this reason: he wrote a book about the whole Seabee Corps, detailing the fact that there were 247 battalions, they had built 12,000 thousand miles of roads, had been stationed at 375 areas around the globe, had 84 deaths, been awarded 700 purple hearts, 400 bronze stars - but not one word of how the job got done.

Q: This was while the operation was still underway.

Capt. T.: Yes, as a matter of fact this was before Okinawa.

Q: Did this have the imprimatur of the headquarters in Washington?

Capt. T.: Surely. In fact, he was the historian assigned to the Civil Engineer Corps, but his was a summary - that's all.

Q: In other words it lacked depth.

Capt. T.: It lacked everything. We felt, however, that our story was a really down-to-earth story about how the job was done from day to day.

The long and short of it was that my friend reluctantly turned me down as Doubleday felt there wasn't a market for two stories about Seabees at the same time, even though they were entirely different.

Q: Actually, Sir, you weren't daunted by this turndown at all.

Capt. T.: I wasn't daunted because I had been very closely associated with it, knew its worth, and could foresee its future value, not only from the point of view of the Navy's accomplishments, but for men themselves. I was concerned that they should have something that they could take home as a result of their efforts.

So I made inquiries of several other companies. I wasn't able to go to see them, but I did this by telephone. I didn't receive any encouragement.

And so we made the decision at that point to spend our own welfare money. We had accumulated four or five thousand dollars in our welfare fund at that point, and the book was to cost us about eleven thousand dollars by a private publisher. We figured that we could sell the books for ten dollars a piece and we would easily make out.

So we contacted and contracted with the Army-Navy Publishing Company in Baton Rouge, Louisiana, which company was making a speciality at that point of printing stories about the armed forces. I then discovered that a great many of the units were writing stories about their own activities.

Actually, we got the book out in about a month's time, which was quite remarkable. The boys bought their copies for ten dollars a piece, and it became a very important part of their history.

Incidentally, I want to go back just a little bit. In our passage back to the United States I had an individual portrait made of each man - the same size portrait, same background, same setting - using our company photographer. Each man had an inch by inch picture of himself in the book, which was quite unique as most of the pictures that were taken of groups were taken of twenty or thirty or forty or five hundred in a picture. Like everything else, a man's face is about as big as the head of a pin. But in this case we published the individual portrait of each man taken with his cap on or not and clean shaven, and underneath his full name and nickname with rank and so on. Then in the back of the book we published a full roster including name, nickname, rank, and home address.

In addition to that we published a dozen or more letters from the various commands that we worked for and worked under, describing in a little detail what work we had done for them and how much they had appreciated our efforts.

In the beginning of the book I re-printed a letter of appreciation from Admiral Morrell, Chief of Bureau of Yards and Docks, and a letter also of commendation from Admiral Studdard who was the regimental commander that we worked for during most of our period on Guadalcanal.

Q: Did you retrieve the welfare funds that were advanced for the publication?

Capt. T.: Oh yes, we almost made money on the book. I think we sold 1000 books or something like that.

Q: Would this be an appropriate time to ask you about the welfare fund - how was this organized, and what you did with it, what was it's purpose really?

Capt. T.: I think I told you at the beginning about the

hamburger stand, where we started making money as a by-product of the sale of Liberty Bonds. We accumulated quite a bit of money in addition to the money that was subscribed to Liberty Bonds while we were out there, and then one way or another we made additional money. As I said, when we came back we came back with four or five thousand dollars or more.

Part of the preparation for our second tour out in the Pacific was to buy with the bulk of our money those things which we had learned from experience would be the most valuable to us for another tour.

A great need we felt was for vegetables. And we had experienced most luxurious growing conditions in the soil - it was fantastic. And we felt that if we could obtain seeds we could grow tomatoes and onions and beans and things of this kind to supplement our diets.

In addition to that we wanted to get some fish nets because we had two or three commercial fisherman in our group who had had experience in commercial fishing in Florida, and we felt it was a shame not to be able to take advantage of this talent.

So we bought considerable quantities of seeds of all kinds, including the order that I placed with one of the seed houses in Los Angeles for one hundred pounds of onion seeds, among other things.

I returned to the battalion in San Francisco and in about a week the delivery came with $2800 C.O.D. bill for one hundred pounds of onion seeds. I had never raised an onion, I knew nothing about an onion, except how it tasted. It develops that I should have put in for a hundred pounds of onion sets, instead of one hundred pounds of onion seeds. A hundred pounds of onion seeds would feed the whole city of Baltimore for a couple of months! And so I had to somehow back out and return the order much to my embarrassment. We ended up with a hundred pounds of onion sets.

The other seeds were quite modest. I don't think we spent more than two or three hundred dollars on the whole order. Onion seeds instead of onion sets was the laughing stock of the whole camp.

The next important thing was getting musical instruments for a band. We had ten or twelve accomplished musicians on board, but there were no instruments. So we spent about eight hundred dollars accumulating musical instruments, not only for a jazz band but for classical music and had a very respectable band as a result. It was a terrific morale builder for it prompted all kinds of entertainment. A lot of singing talent developed that we knew nothing of before. Anytime you give somebody the wherewithal to do something the results are rewarding.

Q: Did other units develop bands also?

Capt. T.: Yes.

Oh yes, the chaplain had a portable organ which we used for bass work in the band.

Triest #4 - 172

Another interesting story about our stay in San Francisco developed around our refitting. During this six weeks period we were there we were completely refitted.

Q: Did you know your ultimate destination?

Capt. T.: No, but we did know from experience that we needed certain very worthwhile pieces of equipment which we did not have. We knew, for example, that we needed more of a certain type of tractor. We needed a great deal more cable because our scrappers were all cable controlled, and we couldn't raise and lower the pans without sufficient 5/8 inch cable. The normal complement of cable was entirely too small, for we were way out in the Pacific where there were no supplies available. We in the Civil Engineer Corps were the only ones using this type of steel cable, so if we didn't have it ourselves where were we to get it?

Q: Wasn't there any overall supply system that would aid . . .

Capt. T.: Let me tell you about that; and this is reverting to my year in Davisville - we had/developed what was known as a table of equipment, much as the table of organization the Army uses for personnel. The battalions were sent out with a certain number of D-8 tractors, a certain number of D-7 tractors, a certain complement of road graders, concrete mixers, quonset hut components, trucks, water distillation units, reefers, and so on. This was all done before the fact, of course. By and large it was fine, but we sent out many too many of certain things and not nearly enough of others. For example, each battalion had two or three reefers, or large refrigeration boxes. It developed that three reefers were too many in that we didn't have enough food which had to be kept cold, and so a lot of capacity was wasted. Of course, each reefer was a large box six feet by seven feet by five feet, and it was a big cubic volume of space that could have been put to better use. In fifty percent of our cases they weren't efficiently utilized. On the other hand they were in tremendous demand by all other Navy, Marine and Army units so they didn't go to waste.

This brings to mind another story of an idea that I set in motion on my way back from Emirau Island. I felt that our complement of equipment needed a major overhaul. So we took the list which comprised some forty odd pages, and in conjunction with every department head went over each single item and decided what we needed - more of this, and less of that. We really re-wrote the entire complement.

The first thing I did on return to San Francisco was to dispatch this to Washington. But I'm sorry to say I didn't even get an acknowledgment. It was five or six weeks work for twenty-five men compiling the data necessary to suggest this revision to the complement of equipment.

However, I'm sure that other battalions had done the same thing for on our second tour the list had been considerably revised, but we got no credit. This was a question I am sure, of somebody's not taking the time to do the necessary, even though a lot of the suggestions were implemented.

One of the things that it was my job to do while in San Francisco was to see that we were actually getting our full complement of the equipment, and trying to help ourselves augment what they did give us as much along the lines of the list we had developed as possible. One of the things, for example, was a decent dentist's chair. The standard chair that was sent out with the battalion was a very rudimentary type, and our dentist felt that he could do much better work if he were better equipped.

The story of the acquisition of our chair is an interesting one that leads to a lot of other things that transpired later.

One week before we were due to ship out, a general order was issued that no battalion would be sent out that was not what was called "dentally complete," meaning that every man had gone to the dentist and everything had been done to him dentally that was necessary so that he could go out and be expected to perform without having to have extractions and other things which might not be possible in the field.

So in one weeks time 1100 officers and men were put through the dental department - some men being in the chair as many as eight hours a day. These boys had come from farms and other comparable walks of life and their teeth were perfectly horrendous - unbelievable. A lot of them had lost teeth, others were just ready to fall out and the cavity situation was something for the book. The extractions that were performed during that period and the new dentures that were made were just a work of super-human effort. These were eighty dentists working on us.

I happened to get one of the best - a chap named Carpenter, and he did a lot of very, very good work on me. I could see that he was one of the brilliant young men in that field.

We had lost our dentist and were waiting for a replacement. When I finally came to I asked him if he'd like to join us, and I found out that his stateside time was almost up, and he would be dispatched almost any moment. So I asked that he be assigned to us. My first question to him was, "What can we do to make your job easier - so that you can be more effective as far as we're concerned?"

Q: You had only one assigned to you?

Capt. T.: Only one, yes.

He said, "The first thing I'd like to have would be a Ritter chair." Ritter chairs were the best chairs at that time and the Navy was supplying those to ships, on more permanent installations, but not for Seabees. I said, "All right, we'll try to get it."

I had my procurement gang well organized by that time. In other words two or three chiefs and others from various departments were organized into a procurement organization. When we needed anything out of the ordinary we'd sick our procurement boys on it and they would go out and somehow purloin it or trade or do something with the storehouse people if they had what we needed and in turn we'd give up something else.

So I said, "Go out and see if you can find a Ritter chair." They came back in about a day and a half with a Ritter chair; we traded ours off to the storehousekeeper. It was an even swap as far as that storekeeper was concerned.

Another thing he wanted was gold for fillings, and he needed a furnace for making dentures. We bought the gold and necessary laboratory equipment out of the welfare fund. We also got extra burrs, polishers, porcelain, et cetera, which were needed to make proper dentures.

Q: You had accumulated sufficient welfare funds for all this?

Capt. T.: We had eight thousand dollars, I believe. I think we spent about fifteen hundred on dental equipment and gold.

The Doc was happy as a clam. Actually he did some very beautiful work. He was busy some eight-ten hours every day.

Triest #4 - 177

I had about eight or ten gold fillings made for myself. Anybody that came in that needed more permanent dental work was always welcome. He got more experience, he told me, in that time he was with us than he would have gotten in civilian life in several years.

Q: How else did you occupy yourselves during that period?

Capt. T.: We did a certain amount of drilling. The boys were busy with calisthenics all the time. We were being fitted for and acquiring new uniforms, and working on the equipment that we had brought back with us that needed overhaul that we were planning to take out again. For the most part they gave us new equipment, but there were certain items that we had earmarked that we wanted to keep, and we were working on them. Then the boys in the plumbing department were busy building oil burners. We were determined we were going to have hot water - instant hot water for the mess hall and showers.

Q: Was marksmanship a factor if you were going to a combat area?

Capt. T.: We went all through that, of course. Everybody went through a marksmanship course, and a lot of boys got medals for their marksmanship due in no small measure to the practice we had had on Emirau.

Triest #4 - 178

Q: What kind of arms did you carry?

Capt. T.: We carried only carbines, and the officers had revolvers, We made a very credible showing on the range.

Of course, there was a lot of liberty during that period. There being no work schedules, we gave as much liberty as possible. For the most part we had a five day week but often reduced it to three or four so as to stretch liberty.

During this period a lot of the boys were privileged to live off the base, reporting only for daily chores.

Q: Did some of them have their wives in the area?

Capt. T.: Some had their wives in the area; others had friends that they stayed with. Wherever it didn't cost any money they took advantage of it.

I personally had a lot of interesting experiences. I met a lot of people that lived there in the Bay area including the De Young family. There were five De Young sisters whom you felt practically owned San Francisco. One of them was married to the editor of the San Francisco CHRONICLE, one of them was one of the foremost people in the historical world, one was married to a prime mover in shipbuilding, and one was chairman of the Bank of America, and so on.

During my stay in San Francisco I was privileged, as were a lot of others, but in my particular case privileged to receive a card to the Pacific Union Club and also to the Burlingame Country Club. I found everybody very, very hospitable.

My new friends did a lot to entertain me, and I'm just not one of these people that takes without doing the best that I can to repay.

So after three or four weeks of this I decided I'd have twelve of my best friends to the Fairmont for dinner. One of the things in the greatest demand out there was butter; butter was in very, very short supply. This particular night I had finagled sufficient points with the management of the Fairmont Hotel to be able to serve a small fillet which was also a rarity.

So we went into the dining room, and I seated myself in a corner of the room with my guests around me. I had brought a paper bag with me and as I sat down I surreptiliously took two bottles out of the paper bag, two pint bottles, one pint bottle of cream and one empty bottle. I poured half of the pint into the second bottle and put the stoppers on. In advance I had particularly asked for butter plates and rolls to be served with the dinner. Then I took one bottle in each hand and sat there shaking the bottles under the table. One after another. Somebody asked me if I had Saint Vitus' dance and so on.

I said, "No, I'm just cooking up a little something." So their curiousity was peaked. I said, "As a matter of fact, (then I raised one hand and they saw that I had a bottle of milk) by my watch in just four minutes we're going to have a little treat." Four minutes added to the five that had gone before made a total of nine minutes. I said, "When I get through we'll have some butter."

Everybody looked aghast. And surely at the end of four minutes clunk, clunk, clunk in each bottle, and I went on for another ten seconds and then stopped and put a snife in and took it out - a chunk of butter out of each bottle which I sliced and passed around.

About a minute later the maitre d' came tearing over to the table and said, "Commander, where did you get that butter? Everybody in the dining room is complaining. We haven't seen butter in months around here!"

Q: Again there's a city boy working to acquire that technique.

Capt. T.: Somebody told me about it, I don't know who, but I decided I'd try it. An absolute neophite for I'd never tried it before.

The sequel to that story is that when I later got married and came to live in Annapolis, I told this story to a bunch of friends here many times and my wife always listened patiently. Finally she challenged me and I did exactly the same thing. I said, "In nine minutes we're going to have butter," and sure enough we did.

Interview #5 with Captain Willard G. Triest

Place: His office in Annapolis, Maryland

Date: Tuesday afternoon, 22 August 1972

Subject: Biography

By: John T. Mason, Jr.

Q: Well, Sir, today we begin Chapter Five. Last time when we broke off you had completed the story of your stay at Camp Parks in California. You had gathered together the necessary amount of equipment and were about to sail in March of 1945 for your next tour of duty in Okinawa.

Capt. T.: Yes, we embarked from San Francisco.

Q: What kind of a ship did you go on?

Capt. T.: We went on a Liberty Ship called the SS _Del Brazil_ and made our first port at Honolulu.

Q: Were you escorted?

Capt. T.: No, Sir.

Q: Tell me about your passage.

Capt. T.: We actually had not only a very pleasant crossing

but a most constructive one. In this period we had an opportunity to review, not only the complement of material that had been furnished us as a general table of organization, so to speak, but also those recommendations, that we had made upon arrival in San Francisco from our first tour, as to additional supplies that we needed for our coming duties on Okinawa.

Q: Did your Supply Officer have it all adequately catalogued for you?

Capt. T.: We had well organized tables depicting what had been furnished to us and which had been loaded on board the ship but, as we suspected, we found a great many deficiencies without which we really couldn't efficiently operate. One of them particularly, for example, was about 8,000 feet of five eighths cable used to operate the tractor drawn scraper pans. We had suffered long days of delay, even months, in our previous operations for lack of cable to operate these pans. There's no sense having tractors and pans available for airfield construction if you don't have the necessary hoist cable.

Q: How did it happen that this item was overlooked at Camp Parks?

Capt. T.: It wasn't overlooked. It was just a question of this requirement not having gotten into the record. The extra cable that had been originally furnished was woefully lacking in quantity. In other words, cable wore out very fast with our 18-hour operations, and it was just impossible to supply it as would be expected of a stateside operation. So that was one thing that we felt we had to augment in some way and going through the list there must have been 75 to 100 different items that we needed increased quantities of - and so I organized my supply boys and some mechanics into foraging parties, each one being responsible to look after his own particular requirements. The man in charge of equipment maintenance, for example, looking after his cable and tractor and crane spare parts; the commissary man looking after the things necessary to help his commissary operate successfully; the electrician needing more electrical wire; the carpenters more nails, and more plywood for forms and . . .

Q: Did not the Hawaiian Islands offer only a barren prospect for augmenting such supplies?

Capt. T.: They didn't offer a barren prospect really for as you know they had vast supply depots with material of every sort.

Q: Did you have access to them?

Capt. T.: No - but we gained access to them by virtue of swapping a little here and a little there for some of the surplus we had. We also had some pretty fast talkers in our crew.

Q: These were supply depots under CinCPac?

Capt. T.: Under CinCPac, and under the Army. Fortunately, we were able to develop a great rapport between our boys and theirs. I'm sure they realized that when we came to them with an urgent request, it wasn't just an idle gesture, we were really in need of that particular material. Well, anyway, during the five days that we were in Honolulu we were able to accumulate most everything that we wanted, and needed to carry on successfully in Okinawa.

Q: So this was all incorporated into what you had already put on board ship?

Capt. T.: Correct.

Q: Who on CinCPac's staff was useful to you in this effort? Was General Leavy there?

Capt. T.: I can't recall the name really of anybody from CinCPac that we ever approached because we knew that if we did - if we approached the matter from a high echelon point of view that there would be a great deal of paper work back and forth and we –

Q: Preferred the direct method?

Capt. T.: We'd end up by losing out entirely so we used the direct method, as you suggest, and from supply officer to supply officer, supply sergeant to supply sergeant type of thing, and we found this was very, very effective. Needless to say, the boys had a terrific time in the five days in Honolulu.

Q: Was there any kind of organized entertainment or was it just every man for himself?

Capt. T.: Well, there was a lot of USO entertainment at that time and a lot of Red Cross girls were putting on shows and were being very helpful, but the boys generally foraged for themselves and were very happy with their sojourn there.

Nothing further of any particular moment happened then until we –

Q: By that time you knew where you were going didn't you?

Capt. T.: Oh, by that time we knew. Actually, I knew and one or two of my officers, but we weren't permitted to tell because the mails were still open and even though we had censorship, the word could easily have leaked out.

Q: Were you made aware of how you were going to fit in to the total operation?

Capt. T.: No, we had no inkling whatsoever; none. We just knew Okinawa - that's all.

On May 1, 1945 we arrived in Okinawa and anchored in Buckner Bay.

Q: Did you, may I ask, how did you get there - did you go in convoy to Okinawa?

Capt. T.: We did. We went from Honolulu in convoy, stopping briefly in Ulithi en route.

Q: What kind of an escort did you have?

Capt. T.: We just had a couple of destroyer escorts and about nine to twelve ships. We anchored in Buckner Bay and the second ship carrying our supplies was anchored immediately abreast of us. The landing itself was uneventful inasmuch as we weren't under any kind of siege. My exec and I went ashore to get our instructions and the lay of the land. We reported to Captain Bissett who at that time had moved forward to Okinawa and was the Regimental Commander on Okinawa - five to six or eight battalions formed a regiment.

Q: But what portion of the island was secure by that point?

Capt. T.: The northern half of the island had been secured and our troops were pushing - our Marines were pushing the Japanese southward carrying the Ryukyuan population with them.

On the - during the first night of our anchorage in Buckner Bay we had one incident which could have been very serious but fortunately was not. A kamikaze came in aiming directly for our ship. He missed us by inches and landed between our ship and our supply ship which was anchored 100 yards off our port beam. Quite a shakeup but fortunately we didn't suffer any damage.

Q: It could have knocked out your whole -

Capt. T.: It could easily have knocked out the entire battalion.

Q: This was your first experience with a kamikaze?

Capt. T.: Well no, we had one experience back in Tulagi when, as I described, one of our boys shot a kamikaze pilot through the head. But, it didn't strike us - it didn't come close to home at that time for he hit the water about a quarter or a fifth of a mile from our camp and only a few of the boys saw it happening.

Q: And it wasn't really a known technique at that point in -

Capt. T.: No, that's correct. In Buckner Bay it was about dusk but still light enough to see. The plane came almost straight down and, as I say, missed our ship by inches - literally by inches.

Q: It came from above not -

Capt. T.: No, he came from above and because of the dusk missed us, as he couldn't correctly gauge his pullout.

When we got ashore we were faced with very explicit instructions, as issued by the Naval Operating Base at Ishikawa. The Commandant having been on the island about two weeks had learned a lot about what happened ashore when fresh troops landed and he issued very explicit instructions about where we should go and what we should do, and how we should take care of our belongings, and the guard setup that we should maintain. Necessity being the mother of invention, however, and the shortages being what they were, it was everybody for himself. Anything that was left unattended was appropriated with dispatch by some sharp eyed Marine or G.I.

Q: Now was this a somewhat separate and different situation from what you'd known in Tulagi?

Capt. T.: Yes. It was a smaller family on Tulagi and Guadalcanal by far, and it was earlier in the war, and I think the commanding officers in the various units had better control, but when we landed in Okinawa with tousands of men - literally thousands of men running back and forth all over the place, and the traveling conditions being as difficult as they were. It had been raining solidly for a couple of months and we literally waded through mud a foot deep, so that just survival was a very difficult problem, and it was so easy to lose something, or to fail to be able to get it to your camp because you couldn't get transportation. The trucks and Jeeps were bogged down, and when the stevedores brought personnel gear and cargo ashore it was dumped wherever it was most inconvenient. Our stuff, even though we had attempted to label it clearly for the 27th Battalion, landed on beaches spread a half a mile apart. Of course if someone saw a refrigerator, and they needed a refrigerator and no one was guarding it, pretty soon it just disappeared to the Marines and Army who were notoriously riding on thin skins. In other words, their complement of equipment was very light and mobile and it was not intended for any permanent establishments whereas the Seabee equipment was intended for semi-permanent camps. In this case every unit knew that they were settling down for a long time on Okinawa and therefore wanted to make themselves as comfortable as possible.

Q: At least you weren't subject to pilfering on the part of the native population.

Capt. T.: No, there were no natives around at that time at all. They were all being herded southward as I've indicated by -

Q: What was the advantage of the Japanese herding them in their van?

Capt. T.: I've no idea and nobody else seemed to understand why, but the Japanese literally pushed tremendous numbers of natives, which at that time we understood to be about 400,000, southward to the cliffs at the end of the island. Here many holed up like mice in the cliffs but literally thousands were shoved off into the water to the extent that when we finally were victorious there were only about 240,000 left. Now a great many of them had died of disease, infections of arms, legs and elephantiasis, and so on - the Japs just left these people where they fell. There was no attempt to bury them; no attempt to remove them, and the sanitation problem that resulted was absolutely horrendous. There must have been billions of flies - literally billions of flies. As we went southward we encountered this particular problem. I'll talk further about that as we go along. Let me refer a moment though to our orders.

When talking to Captain Bissett initially, we found that

we had two specific - he had two specific directives for us: One was that we were to build a so-called combat road, later known as Route Number 1, right down through the middle of the island from a point just north of Naha toward the southernmost tip of the island. The fighting at that time was in the region of Naha. This work was to take one company or the equivalent with one IBM card system. And the second important job was that we should prepare to receive the liberated Ryukyuans, or native Okinawans, when the fighting was over and transport these people and resettle them in the northeast sector of the island, which sector had been set aside by the Island Commander as being the least useful militarily. So! And also, we should build immediately a supply depot on a bay (just north of Buckner Bay called Kimmuwan). Well, we started the combat road with one company and the other three companies made their way to the site of the supply depot and began erecting large or storage Quonset huts.

Q: Would you give me some concept of that highway - Route One? I mean something about it's dimensions, something about -

Capt. T.: Highway Route One was a road which we tried to maintain at 40 feet in width - a crowned road of course - and initially the terrain through which we were to build the road had about a foot of top soil on it, a clay and top soil mixture, making it practically impossible to use so we had to remove it and then bring in fresh coral that we quarried with our 3/4 yard Koching shovel.

Q: It had been a road of some sort?

Capt. T.: No, this was a new road.

Q: This was a virgin road?

Capt. T.: A new road, yes. We had learned from previous experience that if and when building a road we kept the road sufficiently above the surrounding terrain, and crowned - highly crowned so that the water would drain off immediately upon falling - that we could maintain a very good and serviceable road, but once we lost the crown, or allowed the water to stay on the surface of the road it became just as mushy and hard to handle as the mud that we had removed. This was a very important lesson that we had learned on Guadalcanal, by building airfields there, that coral is an excellent building material if you can set it up, compact it, and keep it dry.

Q: Now, was the rainfall on Okinawa equal to that of the southern islands from which you had come?

Capt. T.: No, but we got there in the rainy season. In other words, I believe from the middle of February 'til the first

Note: The typist inadvertently omitted #193 when in the process of re-typing the MS.

of June is their rainy season and the rain was quite severe during that period.

Q: Now, where did you get the coral for the roadbed?

Capt. T.: Well, the island there was rather hilly - but there weren't any really high spots. I suppose the highest point is about elevation 70 but this afforded us inumerable opportunities to just dig into the hillside for pure coral.

Q: Then it didn't have to be crushed?

Capt. T.: We put it down straight from the truck and the tractors, crunched and pulverized it so that it could be finally graded with a road grader quite readily and acted very much as our road building materials here act.

Q: How broad a road was it?

Capt. T.: We tried to make it 40 feet.

Q: With shoulders, too?

Capt. T.: With no shoulders. We were lucky to get 40 feet of useable roadway without worrying about shoulders. But, as I mentioned before, one of the big problems was sanitation and from the moment that we landed we knew that we had a hideous problem on our hands. In the first place, neither the Okinawans, nor the Japanese knew anything about sanitation and as a result flies abounded in that area; so much so that our people would have all died of malaria or some other disease within a very short period of time had it not been for DDT. Fortunately, the Army and the Marines had planes that were equipped for spraying, and every day they just traversed back and forth across the island spraying DDT, completely killing all flies. It was so dramatic that there was a line, maybe four or five feet wide each day from the point where the DDT had been effective to the point where the DDT had not fallen, and the flies were lined right up along that line. As soon as they crossed that line and landed in the area where the DDT had been sprayed they died right away. This was our saving grace.

Q: You had an adequate supply of DDT?

Capt. T.: Fortunately, yes. Now, as we built this combat road forward the Marines were just ahead of us - maybe 200 or 300 yards - and we would build 100 or 200 or 300 yards of road a day behind the fighting lines and that road not only served to bring in troops, supplies and ammunition, but also served to allow Piper Cubs to land, for the evacuation of the wounded. This was the first operation of the war in which the wounded had really had some marvelous attention. If a man was wounded in the front line, for example, within twenty minutes he'd be in a base hospital.

Q: You weren't hampered any in your operations by shells lobbing over the line?

Capt. T.: Oh yes, we were hampered and as a matter of fact, as we slept at night, if you put your hand up you'd have a very good chance of getting it shot off. It was that close. But, our boys went about this thing fearlessly. Whether they were fatalistic or not, I don't know. It didn't seem to hamper their work - we had some dare-devils driving those bulldozers - absolutely fearless, just unbelievable boys.

Q: Did the Japanese in any way attempt to make you a special target?

Capt. T.: No, no. They were too busy with the Marines who were just giving them hell. And, on the southern part of the island where the fighting was mostly concentrated, they had some hills to contend with perhaps a hundred to two hundred feet high. They were filled with caves from which the Japanese artillery bombarded us. They would point a gun out through one of the holes and fire a dozen or two rounds and back the gun back into the cave and then run along inside to another portal, and again fire some more rounds and back it off again and go to another one. Now, we poured tons, and tons, and tons, of ammo into the hillsides, with very little effect actually because -

Q: The hills were honeycombed and with a tunnel. Were these man-made tunnels?

Capt. T.: No, natural honeycombs which were worked on by the Japs to make them useable for storage depots. Actually, the enemy had prepared these facilities long before our assault.

Q: Now, the guns that they secreted in their caves were intended for naval ships, were they not?

Capt. T.: That's right, but they had to turn them to their own defense. Then, as we moved forward there just wasn't enough physical space to accommodate the Japs and the natives and so these people, by the thousands were literally forced over the cliff. Then the Japs themselves finally jumped over the cliffs. They mostly killed themselves for we captured only a few. We then liberated the Okinawans and, by dint of loud-speakers - our language officers were able to persuade the Ryukyuans who were in the caves that it was safe to come out, and to come out, and we'd help them.

Q: Did they understand Japanese?

Capt. T.: No, this was in Ryukyuan. We had some language officers who had been taught Ryukyuan. There was a fantastic language school in Monterey. They could take a man, and in two to three weeks they could teach him a language or at least enough for our purposes. It was just remarkable. And, we had one of these officers in our outfit that we had persuaded the military government command to assign to us. We had great need for him because we were handling all these natives and nobody had any possibility of communication. Well, anyway - with his help and that of about a dozen other language men, they were able to persuade the Ryukyuans to come down out of the hills and let us help them. But, when they came down they were in such pitiful shape that the Army medical authorities, and some Navy too, had to set up operating tables - boards on two wooden horses - right there at the foot of the cliffs and operate amputating arms and legs right there. It wasn't safe to move them and the people were so badly infected and in such poor physical condition that all they could do was amputate and fill them full of penicillin or some other antibiotic. They were then put on stretchers and taken to LSTs, which were beached in Buckner Bay, for the 40 mile trip north to a staging point before another five to ten miles overland. I think we had four LSTs at our disposal.

Triest #5 - 199

Q: Now, facilities had been built for them?

Capt. T.: No, no, not yet. This was the next step. The balance of the battalion which had been moved northward to build the Supply Depot, were finished by that time, and were rejoined by the first company which I had accompanied to build the road and all then moved northward and started the rehabilitation program.

Q: May I ask one question about the road. You ceased operations on that when the enemy -

Capt. T.: In front of that last hill, yes.

Q: Oh, I see.

Capt. T.: At the end of the war when we - when the Japanese surrendered - 21 June 1945 - Route One was finished. Then we went back to our major assignment - the relocation and rehabilitation of the natives.

Q: Had you suffered any real casualties while building that road?

Capt. T.: We didn't suffer any casualties at all - not one. I don't think we even had a man wounded, which was very extraordinary. Oh, a correction. We had one man whose name

Triest #5 - 200

was Tippins killed in that action. In his honor we named our camp "Tippines".

Q: He was killed while building the road?

Capt. T.: Yes.

One of the first decisions we had to make when contemplating our new duty was how we were going to do the job. We had absolutely no building materials whatsoever and we had no knowledge really of what the ground would look like. There were no maps that we could use that were particularly useful for our purposes. They were good military maps. They had hill coordinates, and all that sort of thing, and were useful for artillery purposes but of precious little use as far as our requirements were concerned. We had been advised that we would have to provide for about 240,000 people, and our objective was not only to put them under cover but to put them under cover in some place where, in the future, they would have an opportunity to rebuild a life for themselves. In other words, plant their own produce and farm it, and fish, and so on, so that the groupings of these people wouldn't be unbalanced. Our first job was to make a rough survey of the whole northeast section of the island which is about 30 miles long and about half a mile wide and decide that we could put 5,000 people here, and 20,000 people there, and 25,000 people here, and 15,000 people here, and so on, trying always to give each person or family from a tenth to a fifth of an acre that they somehow could eventually farm.

Q: But it was envisioned that they would be deprived of the balance of the island?

Capt. T.: For some period; we didn't know how long. The soil for farming was excellent and if seeds could be provided they could look after themselves. They were perfectly willing and capable of doing so. In other words, by planting beans and potatoes and rice, and so on, they were able to do very well so our task was to put them in places where there was arable land. Now, in establishing these campsites, or villages - we had to start with some kind of building materials and so we foraged the island and took down every native hut that we could find, all of them being within the military area but unused by our forces. In other words, they were homes or shacks that the natives had used over the years. They were generally made from three by fours and four by fours and four by sixes - very sturdily built - and we decided that the only way we could build anything in the way of even temporary houses in quantity for these people was to re-manufacture the lumber we acquired by the razing of the old buildings. In other words, we would take a four by four and saw it up into four pieces of two by two, and a three by six - we'd saw it up and make two by twos and one by threes and so on, for various purposes. We designed

Lumber resurrected from torn down buildings

Remanufacturing lumber for houses

a typical twelve by twenty-four foot building which was made from three frames one at either end and one in the middle joined together by roof joists or purlins. We used the one-by-threes for joists and two-by-twos for uprights. Then, because of the strong winds, we decided we'd have to anchor the frames in some way, so we dug down about fourteen inches and, nailing a two-by-three horizontally to the vertical member and buried it in the ground. Eventually we ended with six posts in the ground with anchors attached. And then by means of X-bracing, tied the frames together. For nails we used the nails that we reclaimed from the old buildings. Before the lumber was remanufactured we pulled nails. We set up an assembly line of about 40 women in one place, for example, and pulled every nail out of every piece of lumber that we remanufactured, and straightened the nails for reuse. Remember, we had no materials ourselves.

Q: These were Japanese-made nails I believe?

Capt. T.: That's right. And then we set the women to harvesting the rice stalks. They brought these in on their heads, and a few old men, using some of the rice stalks, with their hands and feet plaited rice rope. We ended up with rope - about three eighths of an inch thick - and green when it was plaited. When it dried it was almost as strong as a manilla rope and straw colored. We cut it into 18 inch lengths and bound the

Drilling holes for foundations for building frames

Buildings going up - most did not have decks

Roof structure being applied to frames

Thatching

thatching - rice stalks bundled together into thatches. A single thatch was about three inches in diameter at the stalk end and was securely tied together like a bouquet of flowers. Then with the rice stalks laid flat each thatch covered the equal of two square feet. And these were laid on the purlins with the butt ends up and secured so that we had a very respectable thatched-roof house.

Q: Was this a new technique or had they done this before?

Capt. T.: No, this has been done for thousands of years. The Japanese hadn't done it. They, for the most part, had built the roofs of their houses of clay on lumber with some thatching mixed in with the clay.

Q: Since you talk about what the natives did to help you, you might tell me the readiness with which they cooperated with you.

Capt. T.: We had the greatest cooperation. We had absolutely no problem with the natives. What we did was to give each of our boys a gang of twenty, and in that gang of twenty he had a honcho. A honcho is a foreman, or leader. Each gang consisted of about fifteen or sixteen women and four or five older men - there being no middle-aged people whatever. The Japanese had taken all the middle aged people and pressed them into their service.

Q: Women too?

Capt. T.: No, they didn't take any women. The women were there of all ages but the men started about - well, they looked to us to be about seventy but I guess they were about fifty. They were emaciated and sickly, worn-out people, terribly undernourished as they had been existing on just a bowl of rice a day apiece. That was about the extent of their nourishment. In some of the pictures that I have here in my collection you will see piles of lumber that had been brought into camp from the buildings that we demolished. Here we have a Japanese saw mill that we resurrected being operated by half a dozen Ryukyuans shoving pieces of lumber - four-by-four lumber through making two-by-three and two-by-two pieces. (This is called remanufacturing.) And here we have pictures of the buildings with their A-frames and the middle frame, the purlins on top and the thatching going on, as I've described. Then we had the old men make so-called rice curtains woven from rice stalks or reeds. These curtains were used as walls or partitions in all buildings. Attached to each building was a cookhouse - about 3 x 5 feet. Each building was intended to accommodate a family of 12 on each side, so there were -

Q: Twelve by twenty-four?

Capt. T.: Yes. There were twelve on each side of a two family house so there were twenty-four people in a 12 x 24, and that house had one cookhouse for the twenty-four people. Then, came community sanitation. We took a back hoe and dug slit trenches away from the living areas and covered them with boards - with holes in them - much as the Chick Sales our forefathers used. Fortunately we had enough lime so that we could keep the latrines or benjos as they were called fairly decent.

Q: Did they know this technique?

Capt. T.: No, indeed. When we first got there the natives huts had holes in the corner of each room or maybe one per house. When they were filled they took that material out and used it as "night soil" for fertilization. This was a constant source of infection because the flies would just grow like Topsy on this material. When we got there we had to stop that and we did it with DDT. Also, prior to our arrival there was no segregation of male and female. If they didn't attend to themselves in their houses they just squatted wherever they were. When we built benjos and they were segregated, we enclosed them with matting. In order to teach the natives how to use this new device we had to enlist some of the older people as honchos or special police. It was extraordinary: each honcho was instructed what to do by a language officer, and then he'd police the area. He would walk up and down the line with a switch, and if somebody wasn't hitting the target he'd just use a little switch on the rear end and make them move over 'til they caught on. Within a couple of days why, they'd move up right into line and we had no trouble from then on.

Q: Well, were they then - did they have access to this eventually for night soil again?

Capt. T.: Yes, they did, but it had been treated to a certain extent with lime, but lime, of course, is still good for the soil so we didn't destroy anything.

Q: Harkening back to your wooden frames, and so forth, were you not infested with termites on that island?

Capt. T.: No, Sir, not that I know of. Now, each of these camps we set up a military hospital facility and, as demonstrated by some of the pictures that I have here we quickly trained some of the native girls to act as technician assistants. Here in one particular picture you see a technician giving one of these poor devils an injection prior to his being operated on by the dentist. They learned quickly. It was truly remarkable how fast they caught on to what we were doing, and even though this fellow is grimacing mightily, as you can see, there was no rebellion, nor revolt, and no shying away from it. They marched right up like soldiers and took what we had to give them.

Q: He knew his toothache was going to be taken care of.

Capt. T.: That's right. And very shortly the word got around that we were not going to kill them, that we were going to help them. We also set up an orphanage and found literally hundreds and hundreds of kids, anywhere from one to eight years old that had no parents, and they had to be taken care of so we set up the orphanage and had calisthenics and gave the kids as much food as we could muster. The changes were miraculous.

Q: Amazingly - perhaps you can comment on this. The Japanese had occupied the islands for years and they were cognizant of sanitary measures. Why hadn't they incorporated some of them in the islands?

Capt. T.: I haven't any idea. My only thought is that they probably had more use for food in Japan and for their troops and they couldn't spare any to use among their native populations such as the Ryukyuans. They were spread pretty thin of course down through the Philippines, and so on and my guess is that their supplies were taxed to the limit. Also, Japanese sanitation was no better than that of our natives.

Q: At that point but, they had been there for some time before the war.

Capt. T.: Well, I don't think that they paid much attention to the native life there. All they did was to exploit them from the point of view of personnel and what food they could get. They commandeered everything that they could lay their hands on, and took every able-bodied man there was to press into their own service. I don't think that they cared one whit what happened to the people nor did they do anything to further their living standards. Certainly the houses, roads, water supply, and sanitary conditions all indicated that there was precious little concern for the natives.

In establishing our camps as we went northward, with this system of trying to give each group sufficient acreage on which to live, we had to build a military road since the cow paths that existed beforehand were inadequate for our trucks. We carved a roadway ranging anywhere from twelve to eighteen feet in width out of the side of the terrain, until we got to one point where there was a real horse-shoe bend around what would normally be called a fjord. It wasn't a fjord in the sense that there was much water there, but it was a fjord in the sense that the hillside came right down in a sharp, sharp radiant to the bottom of the valley at sea level. We decided that there was only one way to do it, and that was to build a road across the water. To do so we dismantled four Japanese sugar mills, that had been in operation over the years, and took their boilers, and laid them across the bottom of the stream welding them together to make tubes or culverts that were roughly five feet in diameter by sixty feet in length. We laid four of these strings side by each across the bottom of the river, and then proceeded to cover them with coral to eventually end up with a road which was sixty feet wide at the bottom - I mean a dike which was sixty feet wide at the bottom and thirty-five feet wide at the top. In order to hold the coral and to reinforce the culverts, we had to revet the banks on both sides. We set up a concrete mixer to make a cement coral mixture which was then put into empty cement bags (from our hoard). The chief petty officer operating the concrete mixer with his gang of 250 women and about fifteen men in fourteen days, made enough coral concrete to fill and to place about 10,000 bags of this mixture. Then our trucks and bulldozers brought raw coral in and topped the road off. This made a beautiful passageway for our vehicles which otherwise couldn't have been used beyond that particular point. Well, having done this, we opened another fifteen miles of the island on the northeast sector for this redevelopment.

Q: How durable would a road of that sort prove to be?

Capt. T.: Exceedingly - I bet it's still there, if they've maintained the coral without letting it puddle. Coral is a beautiful building material, as I've said before, if you keep it dry.

In that period, I believe that we erected something in the neighborhood of eight to 9,000 houses that I've described, using a total of about 200 Seabees to organize and direct the work of approximately 4,000 natives. The rest of the boys were busy building roads and preparing sanitary and watering facilities. In other words, we built any number of watering holes, by digging wells and by excavating to the point where water could rise to the surface.

Q: Were they subject to the usual diseases we know - typhoid, and that kind of thing?

Capt. T.: I don't recall hearing anything to that effect. One interesting aspect of the whole was the fact that nature will look after - that the people would look after themselves naturally if they possibly can. We had a couple or three very interesting experiences that had to do with fishing. The shoreline of Okinawa, except for Buckner Bay was very flat and sandy - coral sand. On the occasion of a full moon, or a night before a full moon, suddenly the word would get around that there were oyster crabs. As many as 5,000 people would suddenly appear from nowhere and walk out into this very shallow water, maybe four or five inches deep, and as the water receded the sand crabs would burrow in much as we know it here, and they would scoop them up and get enough fish, and consequently of course the vitamin content of the sand crabs supplement to a certain degree the deficiencies that they had in their food. These people subsisted, to a great extent, on shell fish and their offshore fishing.

Q: Did your outfit have to do with their food supply too during this - ?

Capt. T.: We had to transport food to them and, where we got it, I don't know but one of the LSTs was detailed for that purpose. It was used almost exclusively to bring rice to our central beachhead, and we transported it northward and arranged that each person got two bowls of rice a day. And that's all the food that we could give them.

Q: Two bowls?

Capt. T.: Two bowls. I would say approximately. We'd dish out the rice to a pair of waiting hands - as much as could be fitted into the two hands, and they would ball it. It would be very glutinous and sticky and they would ball it up, and after balling it then they would just nibble on that ball, and it would take them maybe half an hour or up to three quarters of an hour - so many were toothless - to eat a single ball.

Q: Approximately a quarter of a pound to a ball wasn't it?

Capt. T.: Approximately, yes. And then, as I say, they had one in the morning and one at night, and that's the extent of the food that we could give them.

Q: It simplified the problem to have just one type of -

Capt. T.: Well, of course, in addition they were foraging potatoes and beans such as the pictures - one of the pictures that I've shown you earlier, where you see what was called their marketplace, set aside for the central distribution of the produce that they foraged.

Q: That implies that in peacetime at least they had a more varied diet.

Capt. T.: A little variety, yes. Now another thing of course about the whole race of people out in that part of the world - the Asians - they had communal baths - they would all bathe in them. Where possible, they had two or three so-called pools, or sections: one where they would soap themselves, whenever they could get any soap - or mud, using mud to clean. The women, for example, would wash their hair in mud and found it the next best thing to soap, then they would rinse it, and with a very crude instrument, comb it.

After we'd been in Okinawa for approximately three months, I should say and having done as much as we could to get these people re-established, or established, in this new area, and the war having just ended, my executive officer and I decided that we'd come that far, and it would be a shame if we didn't go all the way to Japan, so we secured permission to go to Tokyo. And at that time there had just been established a regular ferry service by the Air Transport Command. We had no trouble getting a ride to Tokyo, and arrived the second day of the occupation, which was by the first cavalry of the U.S. Army.

Q: You were Johnny-on-the-spot weren't you?

Capt. T.: Which was an extremely interesting experience. When we got to the airfield at Atsugi, for example, our Air Force was busily clearing runways and cleaning up areas in which to work, pulling aircraft that had been damaged by the bombing out of the way and repairing the runways so that our forces could use them. I don't know how we got that many people there that fast but, we must have had well over 5,000 troops there by the second day. We were quartered in a hotel called Diachi and proceeded to have about three days of sightseeing in Tokyo itself which was quite something. We were impressed with the complete poverty of the people. They had nothing that we had been led to believe that they did have in the way of the refinements of modern living, probably because of the length of the war and the fact that nothing had been manufactured

for such a long period. The Imperial Hotel, which was General
MacArthur's headquarters was still a very lovely hotel, and
the Diet (Parliament House) was an extraordinary building. It
had been spared, and they were showing sightseeing parties
though the Diet the same as we do in the Senate here. The old
guide had obviously been at it for years and when our GIs went
into the chamber and didn't take their caps off he jolly well
put them in their place. When they sat down and put their
feet up on the balustrade, or something, he would change that
in a hurry. In other words, he made them toe the mark. It
didn't make any difference to him whether we were American
soldiers, sailors, or Marines. We were just another group of
visitors as far as he was concerned.

Q: I like that.

Capt. T.: Very extraordinary. We both had sidearms on and
as we walked around town everybody was most respectful. They'd
get off the sidewalk for us, and when we went to the railway
station to board a train for Yokohama a conductor saw to it
that we got a seat and treated us with the utmost respect. I
don't know whether they really knew who we were or not. Anyway,
we weren't Japanese and we were extraordinarily well treated.
We went to a couple of giesha houses with their baths that
you've heard about, and were entertained by several dignitaries
in town, in return for which we drove them around in a Jeep.

They hadn't been in a car for a long time.

In short, we thoroughly enjoyed ourselves and saw a little bit, at least, of what life in Japan was like.

When I got back to Okinawa, I thought I would immediately capture my impression of our visit and wrote a story called "A Birds-eye View." Correction - a story called "Japan the Unholy: A Birds-eye View", written on Okinawa Shima, Ryukyu Retto, 22 September 1945. And, if you think it appropriate Dr. Mason, I'll read a little bit of this story. It's just one impression gained by somebody who's not an author, and makes no such claim. It is an impression of an ordinary citizen who happened to be a military officer.

Q: And who was there on leave immediately after the occupation.

Capt. T.: Then, unlike many other observers, I feel that the Japanese, not we, have won the war. We have destroyed their air power. We have sunk their fleet. We have disarmed their army. We have burned out the filth they call their homes. We have destroyed two cities, and we have occupied their homeland. All these yes, but they have won the war. In the three cities which I have just visited, Tokyo received the most benefit from the war, Yokohama the second, and Yokosuka the third, et cetera.

Q: Back to Okinawa again. The balance of the story will be incorporated in the text.

Now, you came back to Okinawa, and you were there for some time?

Capt. T.: Immediately upon our return we found that they had suffered a most devastating typhoon. It had flattened our camp and the supply depot that we had just established - some ten Quonset storage huts. It had washed some fifteen or sixteen of our ships up on the shores of Buckner Bay. It had destroyed a couple of hundred airplanes, and generally caused the most horrible devastation that you can imagine.

Q: What had it done to all the complex of houses that you had erected for the natives?

Capt. T.: Surprisingly, the course of the typhoon that had gone through there had mercifully spared a great portion of the area that we had resurrected. I think that they suffered least damage of any part of the island. One of the interesting aspects of this hurricane was the saving of a number of black cats - the Navy Martin flying boats - seaplanes, that were painted all black. Their commanding officer was smart enough to fly his planes on the ground. They were tethered to the ground but he put a pilot in each plane and he actually flew the plane into the wind on the ground. When the storm passed, instead of being black, they had been sand-blasted to the extent that every one of them was bright aluminum. All markings disappeared - every plane, bright aluminum.

Q: And intact?

Capt. T.: And intact. As adversity would have it, a lot of the Army fighter planes - the land planes - had just been upended and destroyed.

Q: I wonder where the commanding officer had borrowed his technique for dealing with typhoons.

Capt. T.: I don't know. I think he just had an instinct about it, but his was the only squadron that came through unscathed. In about two weeks time we had repaired - for the most part - repaired the damage that had been done to our particular camp and were busy with other restoration work.

Q: By this time, were you having new supplies shipped to you from Guam, or any depot like that?

Capt. T.: We were getting supplies all the time, of course, and including more food that we were able to distribute to the natives, and more construction equipment. Our construction requirements began piling up, for more headquarters for this group and that, and for further landing facilities, and for supply depots and so on.

Q: What was our concept at that point for the use of the island?

Capt. T.: I think that - militarily, I really don't know but from our observation I judged that they intended to use it much as they were using Guam - as a staging area and as a supply depot. As a point from which to carry on the war effort. I don't know whether the bombs that were dropped on Hiroshima were dropped from planes that left Okinawa. I have no idea.

Q: Well, what was our concept of the war for the natives of Okinawa? What did we feel our obligation was towards them, as implemented by all your efforts?

Capt. T.: I really don't know, because you see it was a military government at that point, really, and all we were asked to do was to build facilities. Essentially, of course what we did was to try to make their lives as easy as possible, and to help them rehabilitate themselves.

Q: Which was over and above the building operation itself?

Capt. T.: That's correct.

Q: This was something on the initiative of Seabees themselves, or what?

Capt. T.: Yes, indeed. We did everything that we could, far and away above the call of duty. In other words, we - wherever we saw anything that could be done, did it, to make their lot easier and to help them regain their self respect, their health, and living standards. We continued to build bigger and better roads, and build recreation facilities, not only for them - for the natives - but for our own people, and to improve airfield construction, and campsites adjacent to the airfields, and on and on.

Interview #6 with Captain Willard G. Triest

Place: His office in Annapolis, Maryland

Date: Wednesday morning, 30 August 1972

Subject: Biographer

Interviewer: John T. Mason, Jr.

Q: Well, Captain, Chapter 6 today is going to recount some more of your travels. You had returned to Okinawa and then were off to Korea, and that's what you want to talk about.

Capt. T.: Yes. We had no sooner cleaned up the mess left by the first typhoon - and again, realizing that time was short I decided that we ought to take the opportunity that was afforded to see Korea - or Chosen, the capital, and see for ourselves what the situation was. When Bill Cabaniss, my exec and I asked for, and were granted a few days leave, we flew to Chosen.

Q: This was not a difficult thing to achieve? I mean -

Capt. T.: No, it wasn't, because everything was rather stagnated at that point. The war was over and therfore there was no pressure for military objectives to be accomplished on Okinawa. Also, the rumor was around that we'd be going home very soon. I'm not a writer in any sense of the word, but I'm just a healthy - just armed with a healthy American curiosity, and it was in this spirit that I looked at Korea. I recall that Newsweek magazine had recently referred to Korea as the "Forgotten Country", as "Hodge's hodge podge". And, I say rightly - it was a hodge-podge.

Q: In what sense?

Capt. T.: Well, General Hodge who was in charge - overall charge, under General MacArthur, found the most appalling conditions in Korea that were imaginable. For example, in all of our military government thinking, no plans had been made for the occupation of Korea at all, and yet our State Department certainly knew that there were 25 million people there and that these people for umpty-ump years had been governed by about 700,000 Japanese and -

Q: Ever since the first decade of the 20th Century?

Capt. T.: That's correct and, in true Japanese fashion they had established themselves as the principals of all businesses - in every sense. In other words, the executives of these businesses and utilities and so on were Japanese, and once the Japanese were defeated and run out of the southern part of Korea the country virtually collapsed. Nobody was trained to do anything and, in fact we thought initially that we were dealing with an appallingly stupid people but it actually isn't fair to call them stupid. It was just a question of lack of experience and lack of responsibility that made these people appear stupid. When our forces went northward they were stopped at latitude 38, which was the line established by the Potsdam Agreement, and the Russians just told us that we could go no further from there and we were faced with this fact. We couldn't confiscate any Japanese property to help reestablish the country, or help the people to get started themselves. The Russians for example, at that time had, in the northern sector of the country, about 90 percent of the hydroelectric power generation ability, and they just threw the switches at the border line. The southern part of the country was relying almost completely on the northern sector for its power. So, when you cut off power to a great segment of a population, why, everything stops. Nothing can be manufactured and the utilities are -

Q: Even in an undeveloped country?

Capt. T.: Exactly. And so when General Arnold, under General Hodge, established his military government he was faced with an absolutely stupendous job. He found, as I've described, that the companies - that all of them had been run by the Japanese for so many years that there were no Korean executives that were qualified to take over, and so he had to put American officers in as officers of these various companies to try to get something going. His problem, of course, was further complicated by the fact that at least 75 percent of the raw materials that were used in manufacturing in the southern part of the country also came from the north, and that was shut off by the Russians. In fact, the Russians not only shut off the supply of raw materials but confiscated those materials for their own purposes and took them to Russia.

Q: It was a rather unfortunate agreement we made at Potsdam, wasn't it?

Capt. T.: It was a perfectly abysmal failure as an agreement from the point of view of protection of our rights. We just had nothing to go by whatsoever. Of course, I think at that time we all knew that the Russians were taking everything that they required, and giving nothing. Of course, the whole Potsdam Agreement, having been worked out by President Truman, was a most unfortunate business because he was - he and, truthfully, the whole country was completely uninformed as to circumstances in that part of the world and therefore, when we were faced with the reality of the terms of the agreement, we were powerless to help ourselves. Another point that was deemed extremely important at that time was the fact that while this Potsdam Agreement was started between Churchill and FDR, wasn't it at that point? Yes, and Stalin, and shortly FDR died and Mr. Truman came into power. Almost simultaneously

Mr. Churchill was defeated and Mr. Atlee took his place. So here were two neophytes negotiating with Mr. Stalin who was a continuing force and contributing to our malaise, shall we say.

I said above that the country was divided into two parts by the Potsdam Agreement, and when we reached the 38th Parallel we found that in addition to the fact that power was generated in the north, by the same token 90 percent of all the rolling stock and locomotives, and other heavy equipment necessary for production were located in the north and were automatically confiscated by the Russians. They even shut off the telephone communication between the two countries. They also had about 75 percent of the coal the country used and which was normally transported to the south. This also was cut off, so the southern part of the country was in a perfectly deplorable state.

Q: Now were you able to observe this when you went back?

Capt. T.: I observed only the results of it, and most of the information that I got, I got from some of the better educated Koreans - and there were a few, of course, that had been trained in the United States and spoke English quite well. We were fortunate to meet some of these people in our early stages of the visit there and have dinner with - on three occasions with groups of six and eight men that were able to converse with. I brought home their cards and their positions, but they've long since been lost. In most of our visits, however, we were accompanied by one of our language officers attached to the military government, and it was through them that we were able to make these contacts and have the privilege of talking to the natives and gaining our impressions. We didn't travel outside of Chosen, there being no travel facilities available, but we observed what I've described as a result of the absolute standstill of everything in the country. One of the interesting factors that I soon discovered was that there were 61 individual and completely separate political parties in Korea. Sixty-one! Imagine it! And, of course there was no strength in any of them by virtue of their lack of communications and lack of leadership. In a story recently that I wrote about my visit to Korea, I say, "In other words, nobody trusts or believes in anyone - anyone else - presumably for the reason that they have never had a form of government where responsibility amounted to anything. How in the world, therefore, can they be expected to govern themselves?" It meant simply this: that we would have to institute whatever form of government we would and keep control of the government until the Koreans have been educated to take care of themselves. It's going to take a long time.

One interesting factor was that the doctors - and they were among the better educated people - had already, through their contacts in the United States, arranged with the Rockefeller Foundation to send ten of their English-speaking doctors that they had to the United States for postgraduate courses here. This was even before they were able to get on their feet, but they had enough sense to know that they'd have to get some medical education if they were going to take care of the needs of their country because the Japanese had been doing this prior to their defeat.

Q: When you talked with the various Koreans who were educated and well-informed, did you get the impression that they felt they were ready for a Democratic government?

Capt. T.: On the contrary. They were the ones that told me that they were not ready - completely not ready, in any sense of the word - and they went on for hours at a time to discuss their various industries and they'd say, "Well, now look, such-and-such an industry has been run by the Japanese for 25 years and we happen to know that there's nobody that can take over. No trained technical personnel, either administratively or productionwise." And, another thing that they did was - to issue currency in the amount of millions of yen and paid their workers for six months work in advance, so that when our people tried to get their businesses organized to carry on production as best they could, they found that nobody wanted to work. They all had more money than they knew what to do with. This, of course, was a frightful condition from the point of view of morale. They all felt hopeless, and helpless, and as long as they had money, and could use it to buy what little was available they were perfectly satisfied. In other words, there was a general slowdown of operations.

Q: Well, does that say that their national spirit had been killed? I mean they didn't have -

Capt. T.: Temporarily they were just a beaten, beaten down-trodden people. And, as a matter of fact, in the beginning of the article that I wrote about it, I called it, "The Forgotten Country."

Q: Did you get the impression that our people in command there - General Hodge and his staff, and the rest of them - the military government - felt that we should establish a Democratic system in Korea?

Capt. T.: I don't think there was any question about it. In other words, we've never known any other type of government than a Democratic type and we couldn't understand these sixty-one political parties. That was completely beyond our comprehension. I don't know what steps they took afterwards, of course to implement a Democratic type of government because we left after about three days, and then were shortly thereafter returned to the States whereas the military government stayed on for some years.

I guess that's about all that I can say about Korea at this stage. My visit there was very short and I had to try to take whatever notes I could from talking to the 18 or 20 - the most intelligent people that we'd been introduced to and - I think I've recounted in general what they had tried to tell me.

At that point we went back to Okinawa, only to find that there had been another typhoon in our absence. Not as large as the first one, but equally serious in certain respects, and so our objective at that point - our attentions at that point were directed to rebuilding our campsites and repairing some of the damage the last typhoon had inflicted on the countryside.

Q: Had it damaged the new quarters for the natives?

Capt. T.: As I remember, we had relatively little damage in that area, as I think I've said before because the -

Q: You said so after the first typhoon.

Capt. T.: Well, I think that same thing held true. I think that the anchoring of the huts stood in pretty good stead. I don't recall - I certainly don't recall seeing any devastation in that area, even though there may have been some. But our particular campsite was about twenty miles south of the native living areas, and after we once moved out of there why, we had very little reason to go back.

This about wraps it up, Dr. Mason, and I want to thank you particularly for allowing me to relate, no matter how poorly, the small bit of the saga of a few Seabees in the South Pacific. There are hundreds of stories of course which should be recorded for posterity but unfortunately we didn't fly airplanes or man ships or submarines. Statistically more information should be recorded about this great force - the Construction Battalions of the U.S. Navy - the Seabees.

APPENDIX

to

Reminiscences of

Captain Willard G. Triest, CEC, USNR (Ret.)

Index to Appendix

1. Construction Statistics - 27th Battalion, NCBs

2. Pontoon Cells Used for Girder Bridges - article from ENGINEERING NEWS-RECORD for Oct. 5, 1944.

3. A Meeting with Liberated Prisoners - an article written by Captain Triest, Sept. 10, 1945.

4. Japan, the Unholy - a Bird's Eye View - an article written by Captain Triest, Sept. 22, 1945.

CONSTRUCTION STATISTICS
(Major Items)

Excavation, all work - cubic yards	790,000
Roads, (all classes - miles)	73
Airfield taxiways - feet	3,800
Native lumber - sawmill - board feet	960,000
Native piles, secured, 35' to 90' lengths	720
Docks built (all sizes)	19
Bridges built and repaired (permanent pontoon and timber)	5
Quonset huts - regular and tropical	264
Quonset warehouses 40' x 100'	32
Magazines ammunition and torpedo (20' and 25' x 50')	20
Reefers, 6800 cubic foot	11
Buildings, large timber frame	154
Construction materials depots, operation of	2
Fuel storage tanks, 10,00 barrel	31
Gasoline storage tanks, 1,000 barrel	24
Major repair jobs on 145 ships	450
Propellers changed, large type landing craft	160
Diving hours, ship repair and salvage	2,550

MILITARY STATISTICS

Japanese planes shot down	7
Number of alerts - 5 months - Tulagi area	150
Number of rounds ammunition expended, actual combat	Unknown
Riflemen qualified - 27th NCB-Emirau	
Marksman	370
Sharpshooter	60
Expert	10

CONSTRUCTION LOG

Work projects of the 27th Naval Construction Battalion

NOUMEA:

COMSOPAC

Quonset huts, for officer 16' x 36'	3
Quonset huts, for living quarters, 16' x 36'	30
Radio antennas, erected at Magenta Bay	2
Dock, pontoon	1

ARMY AIRFIELD

Runways, lengthen and improve drainage	Several

U.S.N. MOBILE HOSPITAL NO. 5

Landscaping	
Water tank, erection	1
Quonset huts, for living quarters, 16' x 36'	3
Plumbing, installations in existing buildings	

TULAGI:

ADVANCED NAVAL BASE

Government Dock - 50' x 400', 35' draft	1
Pier No. 6 Dock - 50' x 180', 35' draft	1
Sturgis Dock - 18' x 90', 26' draft	1
Roads, coral sand surfaced, miles	7½
Excavation, rock and sand, cubic yards	55,000
Tanks, 10,000 barrel diesel storage	4
Tank, 1,000 barrel motor gas storage	1
Pipelines and pumping system	
Communications inter-island system	
Barges, 5 x 12 pontoon, with propulsion units	4
Barges, 3 x 7 pontoon, with propulsion units	3
Shore areas cleared, filled enlarged and graded	
Excavation, rock, cu. yds.	20,000
Post Office, 20' x 50' timber framed	1
Red Cross, 26' x 40' timber framed	1
Salvage operations, 30' x 60' timber framed	1
Quonset huts, junior officers mess	1
Theatre, outdoor	1

NAVAL SUPPLY

Quonset warehouses, 40' x 100', with cement decks	8
Reefers, 6800 cu. ft.	3
Quonset huts, 20' x 48'	3
Warehouses, timber framed, 30' x 100'	1
Ice cream plant	1
Supply barge, outfitting of	

M.T.B. Base

Docks, timber	3
Quonset warehouses, 40' x 100', with cement decks	

ARMY QUARTERMASTER

Warehouses, 40' x 100' native type	2
Warehouses, 30' x 60', native type	1
Deck, concrete, 40' x 300'	1
Reefers, 600 cu. ft.	10
Quonset hut, 16' x 48'	1
Fencing, around entire area	

NAVAL AMMUNITION DEPOT

Magazines, ammunition, 20' x 50'	8
Quonset warehouses, 40' x 100', with cement deck	1
Quonset huts, 20' x 48'	3
Building, 20' x 50', timber framed with high pressure air machinery and piping	1

U.S.N. BASE HOSPITAL NO. 7

Blue Beach No. 1 - 250 bed hospital complete with all utilities	
Blue Beach No. 2 - 250 bed hospital complete with all utilities	
Quonset huts, 20' x 48', used in construction	70

MACAMBO:

M.T.B. BASE

Tanks, 1,000 barrel aviation gas storage	8
Pipe lines and pumping system	
Magazines, torpedo, 20' x 50'	5
Quonset warehouses, 40' x 100' with cement decks	2
Clear, fill and grade all shore areas	
Dock, repairs to existing concrete deck	
Pipeline, floating 6", lineal feet	600
Roads, miles	½
Excavation (estimated), rock and earth, cu. yds.	6,000

GAVUTU:

HALAVO SEAPLANE BASE

Tanks, 10,000 barrel, aviation gas storage	1
Tanks, 1,000 barrel, aviation gas storage	4
Pipeline, to Tanambogo fueling dock, feet	2,000

BOAT POOL

Quonset warehouses, 40' x 100', with cement deck	2
Railway, marine, for LCP, LCB, and LCM	1
Clear, fill and grade shore areas	
Piling driven, for landing craft anchorage	24

NET DEPOT

Quonset warehouses, 40' x 100'	2

HARBOR ENTRANCE CONTROL POST

Signal tower and office	1
Mess hall, galley and quarters for 200 men, framed	

Harbor Entrance Control Post continued

Water and electric system for all units on the island	
Quonset huts, 20' x 48'	2
Dock, timber, for picket boats	1
Roads, miles	½
Excavation (estimated) cu. yds.	8,000

BOAT POOL AND HALAVO SEAPLANE BASE

Clear, fill and grade entire island	
Tank, 10,000 barrel, diesel storage	1
Tanks, 1,000 barrel motor gas storage	2
Pipelines and pumping system	
Dock, fueling, 45' draft	1
Dolphins, mooring, for tankers	4
Excavation (estimated) cu. yds.	7,000

PALM ISLAND:

NAVAL AMMUNITION DEPOT

Dock, timber	1
Shelter, ammunition, timber frame	1

TURNER CITY:

BOAT POOL

Pier, coral finger	1
Clear and grade site for a 400 man camp	
Galley, mess hall, quarters and all utilities to complete the camp	
Buildings, timber frame	6

CARTER CITY:

LANDING CRAFT FLOTILLA BASE

Clear and grade site for a 600 man camp	
Quonset huts, 20' x 48' living quarters	24
Quonset warehouses, 40' x 100'	3
Towers, signal, timber	2
Quarters, timber frame	4
Native huts, renovated for living quarters	10
Galley and mess hall, 80' x 80', timber frame	1
Utilities, water and electric	
LCT, outfitting of, as a repari and service craft	1
Roads, miles	¼

MISSION POINT:

11TH MARINE DEFENSE BATTALION

Clear, grade and drain camp site	
Galley, mess hall and all utilities	
Operations room, tunnelled in rock	
Dock, portable, 9' draft	1
Purvis Bay Port Directors Office and quarters	
Landing craft watering point - dam, tanks, pipeline, timber dock and dolphins	
Roads, miles	1½
Excavation (estimated) cu. yds.	5,000

SIOTA:

11TH MARINE OUTPOST

Galley, mess hall and utilities	
Roads, miles	15
Pits, for 90mm guns and radar	5
Excavation (estimated) cu. yds.	25,000

BUNGANA:

11TH MARINE OUTPOST

Galley, mess hall and utilities	
Roads, miles	4
Mounts, Panama for 155mm rifles	4
Excavation (estimated) cu. yds.	15,000

DESERTED VILLAGE:

11TH MARINE OUTPOST

Roads, miles	2½
Pier, coral finger	1
Excavation (estimated) cu. yds.	20,000

OLEVUGA:

ARMY OUTPOST

Naval guns, 6", moved and placed	2

PLUMMER'S POINT:

11TH MARINE OUTPOST

Mess hall and 5,000 gallon water tank	1
Road, miles	2½
Pier, coral finger	1
Pits, for 90mm guns and radar	5
Excavation (estimated) cu. yds.	4,000

PURVIS BAY DEVELOPMENT:

TULAGI

Watering point, dam dock, pipeline and mooring dolphins	1
Dolphins, for repair ship anchorage	4
Tanks, 10,000 barrel fuel storage	20
Tanks, 10,000 barrel diesel storage	5
Pipeline, 12", miles	2
Pipeline, 8", miles	1
Pumping units	25
Roads, miles	5
Excavation (estimated) cu. yds.	200,000
Dock, pontoon, fueling, 35' draft	1
Dolphins, mooring	4
Camp, complete for 250 men	1

SINGSONG:

SHIP DEGAUSSING TESTING STATION

Quonset hut, 20' x 48'	1
Dock, small craft landing	1

GUADALCANAL:

U.S.N. MOBILE HOSPITAL NO. 8

Reefer, 6,000 cu. ft.	1
Laundry, 20' x 100', frame building, with all equipment and plumbing	1
Deck, concrete, 20' x 100'	1
Scullery, 20' x 30', installation of all equipment and plumbing	1
Warehouse, 20' x 50', prefabricated steel	1
Bakery, outfitting of	1
Quarters, 20' x 80', prefabricated steel	2
Wards, 20' x 250', prefabricated steel	2
Main galley and mess hall, reroofing	
Roads, miles	½
Extensive open drainage ditches	
Enlarge generator building and power capacity	

COMAIRSOPAC CAMP

Remove entire old camp	
Quonset huts, 20' x 48'	13
Laundry, with all plumbing	1
Theatre, outdoor	1
Water system and one incinerator	1
Sick Bay, 20' x 48', timber frame building	1
Stockade around vital records building	1
Landscape, entire camp area	

BOAT POOL

Quonset warehouses, 40' x 100'	3
Quonset huts, 20' x 48'	2

HENDERSON FIELD

Compass Rose	1
Quonset warehouse, 40' x 100' with concrete deck	1
Deck, concrete, 40' x 100'	1
Magazines, torpedo, 25' x 50'	1
Area, parking, 2008' x 800'	4
Maintenance of field	1

FIGHTER STRIP NO. 2

Quonset hut, 20' x 48'	1
Incinerator, 6' x 6'	1
Maintenance of field	

RNZAF

Quonset huts, 20' x 48'	4
Mess hall, 20' x 120', timber frame	1

PATSU 1-3

Quonset warehouses, 40' x 100'	2
Quonset huts, 20' x 48'	2
Deck, concrete, 40' x 60'	1

CARNEY FIELD

Tanks, 1,000 barrel, aviation gas storage	9

ROADS AND BRIDGES

Lunga overflow bridge 230', all native timber	
Nalimbu River - replacing center portion of old timber bridge with an 83' clear span pontoon section	
Tenaru River - approaches and piers	
Matanikow River - place main spans of pontoon sections	
Roads - miles	4
Total excavation (estimate) cu. yds	50,000

NOB

Quonset huts, living quarters, 20' x 48'	4

PATSU 1-2

Bakery, scullery and mess hall alterations

VD-1

Quonset huts, 20' x 48'	4

5TH BOMBER GROUP

Quonset huts, 20' x 48'	4
Warehouse, 20' x 50' timber frame	1

CAMP CROCODILE

Antennas, radio	3
Hut, radio, 20' x 20', timber frame	1

KUKUM BEACH

Well, deep water, 432'	1

9TH STATION HOSPITAL

Well, deep water, 510'	1

EMIRAU:

NAB

Clear and drain camp site	
Water supply and electric power systems	
Quonset warehouses, 40' x 100' with concrete decks	2
Quonset huts, offices, shops and quarters	29
Tents, for quarters, decks and frames	15
General galley, mess hall, bakery, showers and heads	
Hospital, chapel, brig, armory, and M.A.A. hut	
Frame buildings, offices and shops	5
Wardroom, heads and showers for officers country	
Pier, coral finger, with pontoon wharf	1
Theatre, outdoor	1
Baseball diamond and basketball courts	

BOAT POOL

Clear and drain campsite	
Water supply and electric power systems	
General galley, mess hall, showers, heads and ship's store	
Signal tower	1
Quonset huts, 20' x 48' offices and shops	10
Docks, pontoon	2

MTB BASE

Quonset warehouses, 49' x 100' with concrete decks	3
Magazines, torpedo, 25' x 50'	2
Magazine, detonator, 10' x 10'	1
Water supply system, 2 wells and 3 storage tanks	
Galley, mess hall, heads and showers to accommodate 1000 men	

MTB Base continued

Quonset huts, 20' x 48' for quarters	28
Quonset huts, 20' x 48' for shops, offices, sick bay, armory and recreation	16
Mess, officers, 28' x 72', timber frame	1
Shop, truck repair, 38' x 80', timber frame	1
Shop, metalsmith, 20' x 50', timber frame	1
Piers, coral finger, bulkheaded at outboard end	2
Docks, 3' x 36' pontoon	1
Tower, signal	1
Baseball diamond and basket ball court	1

BOMBER GROUP CAMP

Clear site
Mess hall, galley, heads, showers to accommodate 1000 men
Access roads

MARINE AIR GROUP NO. 12

Hanger, nose, 90' x 40', timber	1

Clear area and drain 2 camp sites
Water systems, heads and showers

NAVY SUPPLY

Reefers, 6,800 cu. ft.	5

ARMY QUARTERMASTER

Conveyor, mechnized food, length in feet	150
Ice cream plant	1
Reefer, 6,800 cu. ft.	1

LCT AND LST FACILITIES

Dry dock, 6' x 24' pontoon and tender barge	1
Pier, coral finger and pontoon wharf	1

Slip, pontoon, 80' x 120' opening and 6' draft, at Purple Beach Landing beaches:

1. Black Beach - est. excavation cu. yds.	40,000
2. Blue Beach - " " " "	8,000
3. Purple Beach- " " " "	35,000
4. White Beach - " " " "	60,000

Blast coral heads in Homestead Lagoon and Hamburg Bay

ROADS

Class 1, 100' R/W main arteries, miles	7
Class 2, secondary arteries, miles	15
Class 3, service roads, miles	11
Estimated excavation, cu. yds.	36,000

TAXIWAY

Taxiway, airfield - ft.	3,800
Hardstands	13
Estimated excavation, cu. yds.	96,000

CLEARING

Army Quartermaster food depot, acres	12
Army Salvage depot, acres	6
Signal Corps Supply depot, acres	3
Purple Beach unloading area and materials depot	10
Black Beach Construction Materials depot	10
Extimated excavation, cu. yds.	5,000

RIFLE RANGE

Clear and grade a 500 yard range
Install 60 targets and complete range equipment

CEMENT SALVAGE

Devise machinery, salvage and drum, sacks	22,000

24TH FIELD HOSPITAL

Outdoor theatre	1

EMIRAU BOWL

Outdoor theatre	1

MANSFIELD STADIUM

Recreation area - softball fields	2
- volleyball courts	2
- basketball court	1

STOCKADE FENCING

Black Beach Depot, Purple Beach Depot and Navy Supply, ft.	7,000

BLACK BEACH DEPOT

Build, operate and maintain the Regimental Construction Materials Depot

P. T. BASE

Estimated excavation, cu. yds.	75,000

MALARIA CONTROL DRAINAGE

Estimated excavation, cu. yds.	10,000

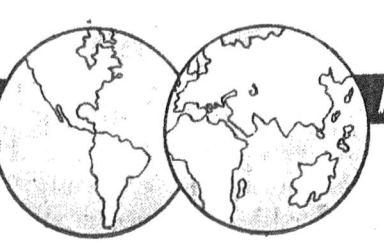

Pontoon Cells Used for Girder Bridges

N. A. Bowers
Pacific Coast Editor, Engineering News-Record

Contents in Brief—*Bridges have been built with the Navy's 5x5x7-ft. steel pontoon cells by two methods; (1) by floating strings of the cells to the site where they are hoisted to place to form a 75-ft. span and (2) by delivering the strings of cells for an 81-ft. span on trailers to the approach trestle, and then thrusting them out across the unbridged span as cantilevers. The principal changes in assembly practice, as compared with that used when the cells are joined to make barges, etc., are to increase the size of the connection angles and to weld the corner plates to the angles. In cantilevering strings of cells, counterweight is provided by filling the rear ones with water and superimposing extra water-filled cells as required.*

EXPERIENCE in applying the Navy's steel pontoon cells to a multiplicity of services (*ENR* July 27, 1944 vol. p. 106) was back of the design of two bridges built in the Solomon Islands, one with a span of 75½ ft., making use of four parallel strings of the pontoon cells lifted into place by cranes, and the other with a span of 81 ft., three cells wide, which was erected by bold and spectacular cantilevering. When the cells are put together in a single row or string, the resultant assembly looks a good deal like a steel box girder, although the designers of these structures, officers of naval construction battalions, say that they are more appropriately figured as Vierendeel girders. Both by calculation and actual test, these pontoon cell girder spans have been shown to be safe for an H-20 loading, with full allowances for wind and impact required under AASHO standards.

Erection by hoisting

As shown in Fig. 2, the 4-cell wide bridge, which was hoisted into place

Fig. 1. Seabees lift a string of eighteen pontoon cells into position to form a girder bridge of 75 ft. main span over a stream on one of the Solomon Islands.

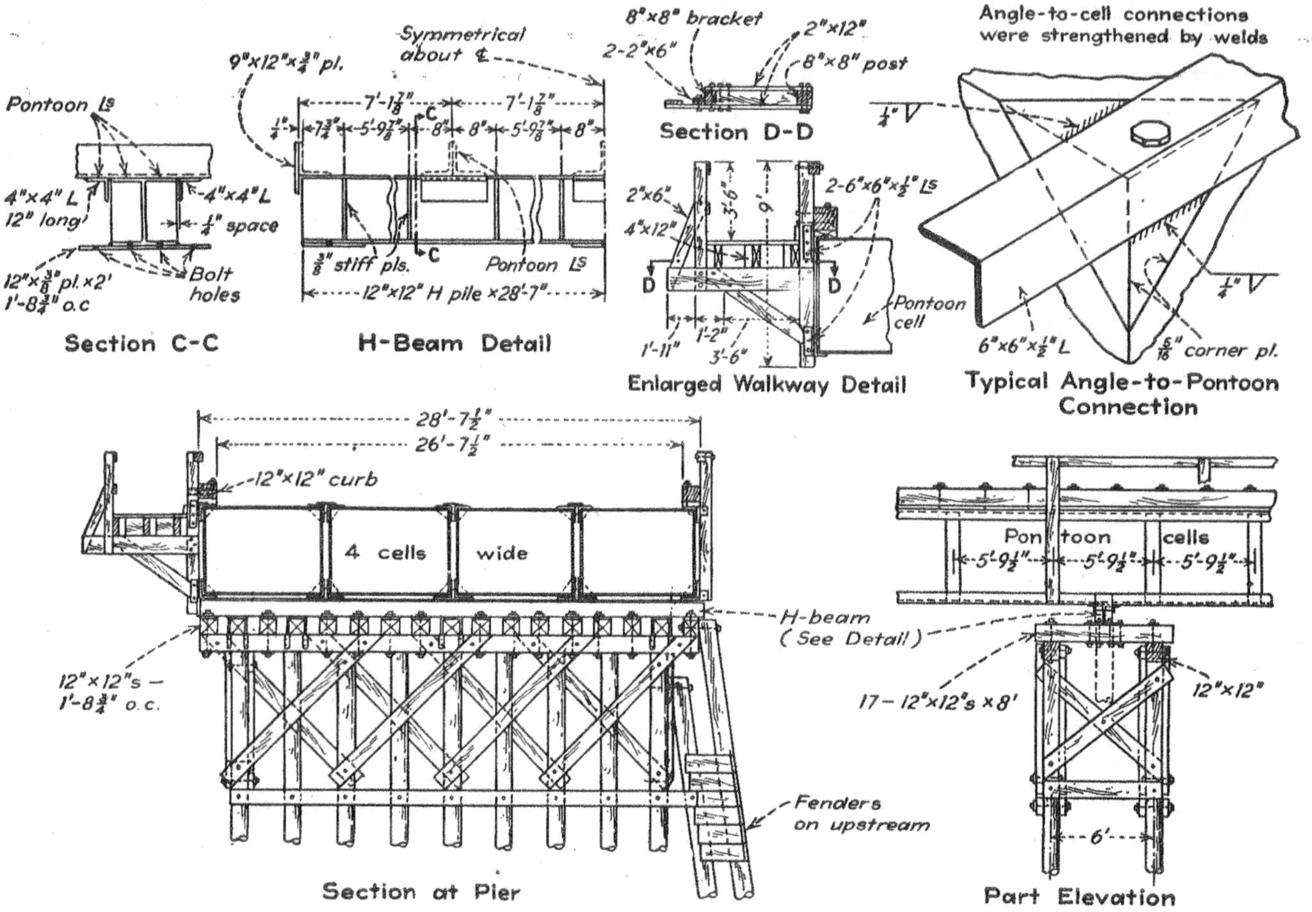

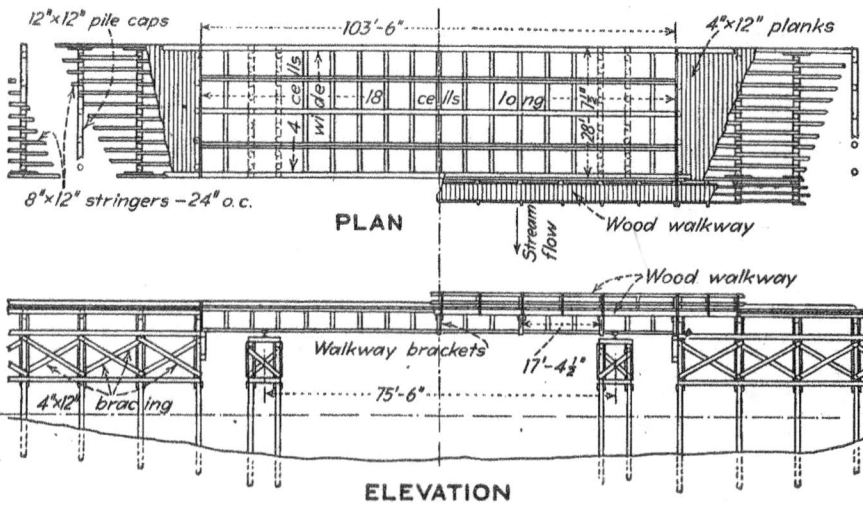

by crawler cranes, is made up of strings 18 cells (107½ ft.) long, which are so supported as to provide a 75½-ft. center span and 14-ft. overhangs at each end. The principal concessions to this special type of service for cell assemblies was to increase the size of the angles that run longitudinally along the four corners of the strings; also to vary the angle sizes to suit the stresses. Thus, 6x6x½-in. angles were used for the first six cells, then 8x8x½ for the next six, while the third and final group of six were 6x6x½. This design works out in such a way as to keep the maximum stresses within allowable limits in all portions of the structure. At the junction of angles of different sizes, splice plates were put on for reinforcement. Finally, as a supplement to the usual bolted-up design that is considered adequate for barges, wharves and the ordinary cell assemblies, the corner plates were welded to the angles. The objective in this was to keep maximum unit stresses in the angles at 15,500 lb. per sq. in. for the condition of maximum uniform load over the entire length of the span.

The bridge was designed by the staff of the 5th Naval Construction Regiment under direction of Capt. A. G. Bissett and was constructed by the 44th Naval Construction Battalion, of which Commander D. F. Thomson was officer-in-charge.

To provide adequate supports for the ends of the pontoon strings, piers consisting of selected wood piles were driven in two parallel rows 6 ft. apart, transverse to the bridge centerline. These piles were very heavily braced in both directions, each row was capped with a 12x12, and across these caps 8-ft. lengths of 12x12s, parallel to the bridge center line, formed a grillage surmounting the timber portion of the pile. To this grillage was bolted a steel plate carrying a 12-in. H-beam on which the strings of cells were landed. Batter piles were put in

Fig. 2. Structural details of the pontoon cell bridge that was hoisted into position. The bridge that was erected by cantilevering is similar, although 3 instead of 4 cells wide and of 81 instead of 75 ft. span.

Triest - 230

TWENTY-SEVENTH U.S. NAVAL CONSTRUCTION BATTALION
A MEETING WITH LIBERATED PRISONERS

by

WILLARD G. TRIEST

Okinawa Shima,

Ryukyu Retto,

10 September 1945

Our war correspondents in the Pacific theater have covered many phases of war. And now, one more phase has unfolded. Not that I am a reporter, but I am going to make an effort to record one contact with this latest phase.

It was Sunday, V-J Day, and, feeling in a particularly thankful mood with my heart anxious to give vent to something, I suddenly decided to accompany Lieutenant Jack Poulton, engineering officer of our battalion, to a camp where the Fifth Air Force is bringing the liberated Army and civilian prisoners of war en route home.

I had one particular friend in mind to look for, Commander Thomas Payne, who was flight officer aboard the USS Houston when she went down in the battle of the Coral Sea back in 1942. I knew no more than that he was alive, the last I had heard in April, and that he had been a prisoner in a large prisoner of war camp just south of Tokyo. In the back of my mind, also, there was the remote hope that I might get some news of the brother of Commander Jack Roulett, whom I had served with for a year at the start of the war. Jack Poulton was anxiously searching for information on one of his best friends, Captain John Wood, C.A.C. officer from Virginia, who had been on Corregidor.

To begin with the authorities are carefully protecting this personnel from a thousand natural questions that they would be subjected to were the military forces of the island permitted to talk to them. I knew generally where the camp was located, but as we rode southward along the West Coast, we passed several encampments definitely designated as belonging to specific units, without finding any sign of our destination. Suddenly we realized that we had come too far, and stopped to investigate. Only after some little time did we find a man who could give us any information. It developed that this particular camp had been carefully camoulflaged by misleading signs so that the natural curiosity seeker wouldn't be drawn to this spot. The MP at the gate was a little hard to impress as he was under strict orders not to follow anyone in. But having come this far, we were not to be put off. Fortunately, I remembered that a Red Cross worker formerly attached to our regiment, was working there, and his name was open sesame.

We entered the Red Cross tent, a mere 17 by 50 field tent, crammed to overflowing with men of all nations: I mean literally men of all nations. There were Filipinos, Australians, British, Dutch, New Zealanders, and many of our boys. To look at their grotesque costumes, you would have thought that Sam Goldwyn had been turned loose once more. Yes, they were a strange group, some with shorts, or shorts and skivvy shirts, some white, some olive drab, some green. Other were better clothed with new Army issue of khaki, some wore dungarees, and some were clinging to the uniform of their native lands. For hats they were all sorts - British tars, New Zealand campaign hats, American sailors that were once white, and liners of American helmets. They were a strange lot, all. Some of these boys had beards, sideburns, and handlebar mustaches. But for the most part, they were clean shaven. I wasn't to understand the reason for this until somewhat later.

As I walked through the tent, I was impressed at once with the filth of the place - paper strewn all over the floor, newspapers, writing paper, wrappers from candy bars, chewing tobacco containers, toothbrush holders, toothpaste boxes, shaving tube boxes, et cetera. The answer was obvious. These men were transients, all, some of them being in the camp a mere matter of hours before their next transportation could be arranged. And not being there long, cleanliness didn't matter; besides, they were too happy with the thought of being alive and among such plenty that a little thing like paper on the floor was insignificant. As I got to the counter at the rear, men were greedily grabbing the cigarettes, candy bars, writing paper, matches, chewing tobacco, soap, razors, combs, and anything else that the Red Cross had to give them. One young chap stood there in a dumbfounded way and asked one of the Red

Cross girls, "Is it really all right for me to take a piece of chocolate?"

I went behind the counter and asked for my Red Cross friend, as I had guessed by this time that getting any information was going to be difficult. He wasn't there at the moment, but I did persuade someone to direct me to a man who could tell me if our friends were there, or had passed through. We went on a little further into another hastily erected tent where we found eight or ten clerks with stacks of papers, a teletype machine, a few tables, and records all over the place. They tried to help us with the information we sought, but pretty soon we realized that the task was almost hopeless. We did, however, believe that neither Commander Payne nor Captain Wood were in the camp. As for young Roulett, we saw that they had no way of telling us, and so that was that. You see, they hadn't been prepared for this tremendous task of taking care of the enormous number of people that were being shuttled into the camp and taken away again in so short a time. Apparently these liberated prisoners just began arriving, and the machinery to bathe, clothe, feed, and interrogate these people had to be very hastily set up. Then shipping schedules had to be arranged, or they had to be put aboard planes bound for Manila and thence on home.

After some time we were forced to give up that task and we wandered around for a few minutes. In the back of a tent stacked with boxes, I found my Red Cross friend. He and several others were sitting on some boxes having a coke and looking very much the worse for wear. It appears that they hadn't been off their feet for some thirty hours - so busy had they been receiving and dispatching a particularly large group. I was introduced all around. The first was a very jaunty Britisher, I would say fiftyish; then another somewhat younger man, who turned out to be a civilian engineer captured at Wake. Jack Poulton came in then, and the conversation drifted back to the topics which they had been discussing.

The Britisher, as I said, was a particularly jaunty individual, jaunty, partly because of his cocked hat. He was a major of His Majesty's Light Anti-Aircraft Artillery. We could see at once that he was proudly clinging to that one little bit of his uniform which would set him off as a British officer. He was Major Charles P. Graham, R.A., of Castle Size, Sallins, County Kildare, Ireland, and had been captured on the 9th of March 1942 while serving under the Dutch in Java. He had weathered the storm and come through very well. To be sure, he was lean, having lost some forty of his 175 pounds, but his eye was bright, and his congenial manner contagious. Actually he presented an extremely funny sight dressed as he was in ill-fitting green, woolen shorts and undershirt, big British Army boots, white socks, his Army cap and cherished pipe. To see him sitting there chattering about the war one would have thought that he might just have been shipwrecked, but you wouldn't guess that he had spent four long years in a prison camp.

The other, Mr. F. A. Knight, was a resident engineer for Morrison - Knudsen Company, civilian contractors building the fortifications at Wake Island when it was captured by the Japanese. Mr. Knight, too, seemed happy and content with the world, but somehow I got the impression that that long stretch as a prisoner had done more to break him down than it had our English friend.

After a few minutes, I realized that probably nothing would mean more to these men than a chance to visit with us, and talk, for it was very obvious that they were starved for news of happenings in the world and just to talk to people of their own kind. I asked them if they wouldn't like to spend the afternoon with us and have dinner in our camp. After a little investigating, we found that they were not going to be shipped out before morning, so we took a chance.

As we were waiting for them to change into their Army issue clothing, Mr. Reid, my Red Cross friend, asked if I could help them in another matter. I was delighted, of course. He said he had a young chap whose brother was in the Seabees connected with some brigade, and did I know . . .

"You don't mean," I said excitedly and with all the assurance in the world that it must be so, "Commander Roulette?"

"Why, yes," said he.

"The boy is Jack Roulett's brother. We must find him."

Shortly, our three new friends were ready. We piled

them into the jeep and were off. I encouraged the major to hide his cap just in case the MP at the gate should get inquisitive and stop us.

From that moment on, neither the major nor Mr. Knight stopped talking any longer than just to listen to the question we had to ask. They were bubbling over with enthusiasm for human companionship which seemed to symbolize their liberation to them. As we rode along, first one, then the other would ejaculate at the size and quantity of construction equipment which they saw along the road, the tremendous number of trucks, the countless campsites, hundreds of ships which lay at anchorage in first one harbor and then another along the road, and the frightful damage and the havoc which had been brought on towns like Shurj and Yonabaru during the last days of the fighting on Okinawa.

We went first to Commander Roulett's camp and stopped outside his tent while I furiously blew the horn. Jack's sleepy voice answered, he was taking his siesta; "Come on in," he shouted. "No, you come out," I answered. In the meantime, I had urged Donald to keep his seat. We were all so terribly keen to witness the first meeting of these brothers. After a few moments and a number of yawns, Jack appeared and slowly approached the car. Apparently he had been sleeping for he didn't grasp the situation. He greeted me, and then his eyes traveled over the other occupants of the car. Suddenly, his brother appeared from behind and, as Mr. Knight said, the look on their faces was worth a thousand dollars gold. Jack's first words were, "Well, I'll be --- !" And then: "You lost your bridge!" Toothless Donald allowed that he had but that it could be fixed.

Jack asked us all in and, "Wouldn't you all like a beer?" That beer, Mr. Knight said, was his first since the day before he was captured, and did it taste good! They each had three promptly.

Some time later, we took our leave of the two brothers, with the promise that they would join us at the Twenty-seventh camp for dinner. My first thought was that the major whom I had more or less taken under my wing and shown to my quarters would like a shower. And so, indeed, did I want one. We lost no time in preparing ourselves. I could see immediately that his forty pounds had been lost around his neck, chest, arms, rump, and thighs, and that he had developed a little pot belly as a result of years of inadequate and the wrong kinds of food. One of his first questions was, "Do you know how you can always tell a prisoner of war?" Of course, I didn't know. He said, "Look at these," and he showed me two large black and blue marks, one on each hip. He explained that every prisoner of war is exactly the same way. It appears that having nothing but the hard ground to sleep on, their thigh bones continually bruise the skin, with the result that these bruises, about three inches in diameter, appear within a very short time and stay with them during the whole period of captivity. I also noticed that he was completely without a rump which, of course, made it most uncomfortable for him to sit on any hard surface. To see the expression of sheer joy spread on his face as he sat on my canvas chair more than repaid me for the trouble I might have gone to in getting him there. Then he told me about the fleas, bugs, and lice. His thighs were covered with flea bites. It seems that during the winter when it is cold, the bed bugs attack in force. In the spring and fall, with moderate weather, the lice are the worse, and in the hot summertime, the fleas take their toll. "It was not uncommon," he said, "to be kept awake more than half the night and then to drop off to sleep so darn tired that no amount of bites, no matter how ferocious could keep you awake."

After a bath and a shampoo, and with a pair of comfortable slippers, the major felt better. We adjourned to the wardroom for a drink.

No, the major hadn't had a drink since he had been freed. In fact, the beer we had earlier in the afternoon had been his first since that fateful day in March, 1942. No, he didn't think that he ought to have any whiskey - beer would do. As a matter of fact, I thought that whiskey would have been better on a week and unfed stomach, but it was his day. As we sat around talking, more officers kept dropping in, and soon the major had a rapt audience. It appears that in February, 1942, he was sent to Java as second in command of the Forty-eighth Light Anti-Aircraft Regiment, and served there for a mere thirty days before the trouble started. The Dutch were in command, of course, and had some 180,000 troops on the island. What happened to them is unexplainable, for it appears that after the first bombing of Batavia which is the capital of Java, the Dutch were so petrified that the colonel in command surrendered his entire force and these British serving under him at the first demand of the Japanese. He surrendered in spite of the fact that there were less than 200 casualties among the entire allied troops. This 200, by the way, consisted of both dead and wounded, but by no means were they all killed. To say that the major and his regiment have cursed them ever since would be putting it mildly. There may have been extenuating circumstances, but as far as is known, nothing more than the familiar Japanese threats.

Major Graham with his twenty-four officers and 750 men were put on a troop-ship and taken to Foukuoka where they were interned in a primitive prisoner of war camp. The trip up, he describes as "vertible Hell". In the hold of the ship in which he found himself, there were 520 men and officers crammed into a space 50 feet by 80 feet, three decks below the main deck. Of course, there wasn't room for more than 75% of the men to sit or lie down at any one time, so they had to arrange their schedule accordingly. Miraculously, only sixteen of his men died during their five weeks' cruise. On a sister ship, one of his officers reported that 110 men had died, plus 200 more within a few days after their landing, as a result of a cruise of the same duration. All of these deaths were due to dysentery, and in the words of the major, "Why we all weren't dead, the Lord only knows." The only head facilities on board these ships were three heads built over the stern on the starboard side and three more on the port side. These heads had to serve 1800 British prisoners, 100 civilian prisoners, plus 500 Nips.

Being interned in the Foukuoka prisoner of war camp was an experience which we imagined sufficient to drive almost any sane man crazy. But we were surprised to see how sane the major was. His spirit, that familiar old time British spirit, wasn't broken, his eye was clear; his voice cheerful, and his enthusiasm undaunted. In fact, instead of being thoroughly disgusted and fed up with the world and everything in it and particularly with the Army, his attitude seemed to be one of "all in a war". In fact, he told me privately afterwards that he thought he would try to remain in the army for ten years or more before retiring. It was tradition, of course, for the son of a rich man to serve in His Majesty's Army. We as Americans found it hard to believe that the days of pomp and ceremony, silver buckles and golden swords are not gone. He said, though, that the days of twenty different uniforms would never return, but he feels that the British will carry on with their military splender and he wants to be part of it.

In the meantime, Jack Poulton, Dean Works, and Johnny Hunter had taken Al Knight on a busman's holiday. In fact, the one thing that Mr. Knight wanted to do more than anything else while he was on the island was to visit the Japanese prisoner of war camp that we maintain here. He wanted to see how it felt to be on the other side of the fence. As they came to the sentry post, they were stopped, and asked a lot of questions, for here again, outsiders were not wanted. As soon as Lieutenant Poulton explained who Mr. Knight was and the circumstances, an officer of the camp called an interpreter and showed them around. As they came in, the Nips were just forming for some sort of exercise and their commanding officer called them all to attention, and ordered a hand salute. Jack and the others were a little nonplused at this, but were careful to watch the expression on Mr. Knight's face. Dressed in Army clothes as he was, they thought, of course, that he was an Army officer, and to the surprise of everyone, he smartly returned their salute. For four solid years, he had been required to come to attention and salute every time the lowliest Nip private had come within range in their prison camp and hold that salute until it was acknowledged. Now he was getting his just reward.

He had learned, the Japanese commands for attention and salute but in no way did he show it. He was full of curiosity and asked many questions about how the prisoners were treated, their hours of reveille, mustering, chow, and so on, and the amount of food they were given. To each answer, the engineer told what had happened to him. His reveille had been at 0430 and the reveille of the Japs was 0600. His muster had been at 5; their muster was at 0630. His breakfast consisted of 130 grams of cooked rice while theirs consisted of 390 grams, and so it went. His attitude was that of the professional prisoner, as compared to the amateur. What an easy time we gave the Japs by comparions.

About six o'clock the sightseers returned to our wardroom and settled down to a little earnest drinking and talking. There was no keeping anybody quiet. Questions would be asked and answered and hardly before one was through speaking, someone would have another question ready. We literally bombarded them. And they loved it. To our surprise, they had little to ask of us. To be sure, I presume they had had too little news to stimulate their imaginations about what was happening in the world or what had happened since they had been away whereas their own experiences were fresh in their minds. They were only to happy to tell us about them.

For the most part, we didn't hear the horror stories that we have been hearing here on Okinawa about the Japanese atrocities. No, they were much more mild, really, but probably because these men were officers and imprisoned for the most part in officer prison camps. What the Nips did to the common soldier not even they knew, but they did have a few facts about their lives in general which I will try to relate.

In the first place, their diet consisted, for the most part, of 390 cooked grams of cooked rice in a 24-hour period. This is equivalent to some three or four ounces, or less than 1/5 of a pound of raw rice. When cooked and made into a ball as it was served to them, it would amount to about the size of one tennis ball three times a day. Occasionally, and very occasionally, they had seaweed soup, which consisted simply of seaweeds cooked in water which extracted the iodine and salt. Occasionally their diet was changed for a whole month and they would get the equivalent helpings of soya beans, or barley. Under no circumstances did they ever receive any food containing proteins.

Now this sort of a diet, cooked rice being 98% water, bloated their systems horribly. It was not at all uncommon, therefore, for every man to urinate eight to twelve times during a single night. In other words, between the bugs and the insistent call of mother nature, honest sleep was a rarity. On one occasion one of the men received a Red Cross package and ate his first tin of bullied beef in a year. The proteins reacted so strongly on his kidneys that he urinated forty-eight times in twenty-four hours.

As we can appreciate, the subject of food and diet and sickness were uppermost in the minds of all of these men. And so we heard everything down to the last detail. The major said, for example, that the most of the prisoners looked fat and, therefore, healthy, but in truth, they weren't fat at all; they were just bloated with water. You could push your finger in the man's thigh, an inch and a half and it would be some little time before the skin would come back to its normal position, so much water was contained in the flesh. "At last," he said, "I now know what a hollow leg is."

Of all the Red Cross packages that have been sent from home, only a small percent were received. For example, during the four years these men were prisoners, they were only allowed three visits by the Red Cross. They came in March, 1943, for the first time; then in May, 1944 and finally on the 2nd September, 1945. It transpires a great many of the Red Cross shipments that were sent over in 1942 were confiscated and were later found on one of the Nip islands, being used by their troops. All of the shipments of 1944 disappeared in some mysterious manner. "However," the major continued, "Had it not been for the packages that we did receive, fully 35% more of our people would have died of starvation."

"As a matter of fact," he said, "I estimate that at least 40% of all prisoners died of either starvation or sickness. They would allow our doctors to treat us, but they wouldn't give them any drugs with which to work. They had a few surgical instruments and bandages, and that was all. How we all kept from dying or going stark mad no one will ever know."

By comparions, it is interesting to note that the Americans have been feeding the native Okinawans fourteen to sixteen ounces a day for the non-workers, plus a C or K ration at the noon meal for the workers.

These two men had so many stories to tell, it's hard to recount them all here. But a few more come to mind. The major said, for example, in showing me a scar which started at his left temple and went around the base of his scalp to the back of his head and then forward across the top, "Do you see that scar? Well, that scar saved me from many a beating. The Nips are funny people. They knew that I received that scar in the first World War. Why they believed my story, I'll never know, but anyway, they did. During the first World War they were our allies and, therefore the wound had been received in the name of the Emperor. Therefore the scar was holy." When the Britisher was in the labor compound, or standing in formation, for example, they would bark, "Ki Wo Tsuke," meaning attention, and "Kei Pei," meaning salute. "Then the commandant with whom I as senior officer present did not agree, would cuff me on the head, being always careful to hit me on the right side of my head, never the left. By the same token, I have a large shrapnel wound in my right leg. They would never kick me on the right leg, always on the left leg. We never could understand their warped mentalities."

Yes, they did tell us one or two horror stories. On one occasion when one of the major's regimental officers died, the commandant of the camp made Major Graham and the others truss up this officer with his knees to his chest, put him in what they supposed was a casket, and cart him away. They didn't know where, of course, until they arrived and saw a crude outdoor furnace. The body and the refuse under it used for kindling was doused with gasoline and the major, as senior officer present, was required to light the match to set it off. After this horrible act, the major was then required to collect the ashes and put them into a box. Purportedly it was to be sent to the officer's family.

The enlisted men were required to work each day in the fields or at some other labor, and were allowed double portions of rice for each meal. The officers, on the other hand, refused to work and that refusal was accented, but during the hours from reveille (pronounced by the major re-veillie,) until taps, they were not allowed to sit down. If a man complained that he was sick, that was just too bad unless he had a temperature of 102 degrees or more. Then he was allowed to lie down. At night in the barracks, they slept on the ground and on shelves just 30 inches above the ground. Each man was allotted 2' 4" by 6', and there was a 3-foot aisle down the center. Can you picture this hell?

Then we were to learn the reason for the relatively few beards and shaven heads on these returning soldiers. It appears that the Jap soldier and officer, being extremely vain people resent tremendously their regulations which require that they're close cropped, and so they vested that resentment on our boys. The Nips (these men always referred to them as

Nips, never Japs) supplied clippers, and in the event that a man was not close shaven, they would grab his hair and pull him around until he screamed with pain. To be treated once or twice like this was enough to make any man obey.

In their camp, the commandant received two Japanese papers printed in English, presumably so that he and his interpreters could keep up with the language. At first the Americans were allowed to buy copies at exorbitant prices, and then suddenly one day they were refused. The major wanted to know why. The Nip commandant, in his surly fashion, refused to answer. Finally, he said that the inspection had not been good the last time, but that if the Britisher would promise to have the camp spic and span for the next inspection of the Nip colonel, then they could have their newspapers again. Inspection day came and the commandant was praised for the good job he was doing but the next day still no newspapers. According to the major, "It took me twenty minutes with the aide of the interpreter to tell him what a 'bloody' liar he was." Finally, after three weeks, the commandant again approached the SOP and told him that his colonel was coming, and wanted a good inspection, but the SOP shook his head and said, "Never again." But the command said, "You can have your papers if you only give me a good inspection." The SOP shook his head and said, "It took me twenty minutes last time to tell you what a bloody liar you were. You think I would believe you now?" Inspection day arrived and the commandant caught hell. He in turn raised hell in his part, but the next day the troops received their papers once more.

According to the major, if you give in to the Nip at all, he instantly loses his respect for you. On the other hand, the more you curse him and the more stern your manner, the more respect he has for you. If you are so fortunate as to be able to keep out of the Nip's way, in other words, if you do not attract attention to yourself, you are, of course, much better off, but, as the major said, "Here was I, the senior officer present. I didn't stand a chance." Some of the men learned the language, or at least enough to get along on, while one young officer made up his mind he would master the subject and in two years became sufficiently proficient to read, write, and speak Japanese. As a matter of fact, this knowledge stood them all in good stead, but most of them preferred to make the Nips speak to them in English, or through interpreters.

In the beginning of the war, the newspapers printed tremendously exaggerated accounts of the Japanese successes. For example, there were the stories of the five battles of Bougainville. Each time, the Japs withdrew, but only after fantastic losses on the part of the Americans. It was nothing for us to lose seven carriers, four battleships, eight cruisers, twenty destroyers, in a single battle. Eventually, though, little bits of truth would come out as the toll of damage mounted beyond the totals of all the world's fighting ships, and bit by bit, the newspapers revealed that possibly the damages inflicted on the Americans were not so great as had been reported. Gradually, it seemed to dawn on them what was happening, they faithfully reported our landings even "though with terrific losses." The Japs slowly but surely realized that they were losing the war. The major thought that by June they realized the game was up, but that never daunted the spirit of the fighting man. The militarist was always the militarist and never willing to consent to any possibility of defeat.

On the other hand, though, the stories of both Major Graham and Mr. Knight confirmed one another in their ideas that the Jap coolie isn't at all military minded. They said that any time they came in contact with a civilian they were treated very well. They would smuggle the prisoners food, tobacco, give them old clothes, let them rest at their work when the soldiers weren't around, and so on. It was the prisoners' idea that the Japanese civilian was not at all in sympathy with the war or the aims of the militarists. In fact, this spirit was somewhat collaborated by our own American officers of the prisoner of war camp on Okinawa. When Mr. Knight and our officers visited this camp, they were shown the Nips on one side of the road in their barbed wire enclosures, and the Korean and Okinawans on the other side of the road in their enclosure. The American officer explained this by saying that there was such animosity between the

Koreans and Okinawans and the Japanese soldiers that if they once got together, the Koreans would tear the soldiers limb from limb. They seemed to be an entirely different breed.

During the whole course of the war, the British Government withheld from Major Graham's pay ten pounds per month which according to international prisoner-of-war regulations was to be paid to him through the Red Cross at the rate of seventeen yen to the pound. During the entire four years, the Nips kept practically all of this money. The Nips charged each man thirty yen per month for his food, then paid him fifty yen to cover his expenses. The balance was confiscated. The interesting part was that on about the fifth of September when the Nips finally realized that the war would be over in a few days, they began to curry favor with all the prisoners. They opened up the food lockers and gave them everything that they could eat. They gave them all the back pay that they had confiscated, and even paid one man ninety yen interest on 4,000 yen which they had confiscated during the four years pariod. As a result, the major left Japan with a great many yen on his person which his government has promised to redeem. I believe he said that he had an equivalent of some 350 pounds.

As a result of this change and the liberal food policy that the Japs adopted just prior to the surrender, a great many of our boys had gained pounds before they were liberated. Both of our guests had gained almost fifteen pounds in nine days. And it was the same with all of them.

Unfortunately, we didn't get an opportunity to talk very much to young Roulett, a corporal in the Army. Here was a boy, roughly twenty-one years old, who had been captured at Bataan. He was badly wounded but was forced to take the "death march". It was difficult for us to tell whether he was still bloated or whether the good food which he had been eating for the past ten days had really brought him back so much. In some ways he had the look of an old man in spite of his youth.

JAPAN, THE UNHOLY

A BIRD'S EYE VIEW

by

WILLARD G. TRIEST

>Okinawa Shima
>Ryukyu Retto
>22 September 1945

Not unlike many other observers, I feel that the Japanese, not we, have won the war. We have destroyed their air power--we have sunk their fleet --we have dis-armed their army--we have burned out the filth they called their homes--we have destroyed two cities--and, we have occupied their homeland. All these, yes; but they have won the war.

In the three cities which I have just visited, TOKYO received the most benefit from the war, YOKOHAMA second, and YOKOSUKA third. In TOKYO I found 95% of the public utilities intact, all the roads, bridges, and harbor facilities unharmed, ninety percent of the modern buildings with little more than a few panes of glass broken, the PALACE, the DIET, and all of their shrines standing as before symbolizing their faith--only the rottenness was burned out. TOKYO was not touched by any demolition bombs, but suffered incendiary raids only. These raids were completely successful. Practically all of the small, vermin ridden, stinking shanties were burned to the ground. In one area practically all of the city's most undersirable people were burned to death. But aside from this and streets littered with rubbish such as would accumulate anywhere in the world where the street cleaning department had ceased to function, TOKYO stands today more than seventy percent intact and a lot wiser from what it has learned.

YOKOHAMA, the great port of JAPAN, seems also to have suffered only too little for the Hell its people have brought. Here, too, I found that only the most undesirable, weakest features of this city had been destroyed, whereas the foundation of the city, the new YOKOHAMA, still remains to laugh and jeer at us.

The great naval base of YOKOSUKA was untouched. But thank God the atomic bomb did its job in the complete demolition of HIROSHIMA and NAGASAKI.

From about the middle of August, the Japanese newspapers and other propaganda agencies began preparing the people for the inevitable surrender, or rather for the treaty, which was to bring peace. In the prison camps, there was a noticeable slackness of restrictions, cessation of beatings, and increase in food. The "so sorry" attitude was once more the order of the day. By the second of September, the people had forgotten all about the war, were telling us that we should forget all about Pearl Harbor and that they would forget all about the atomic bomb--let us all live together in brotherly love. They met our forces of occupation gladly, almost jubilantly. The telephone company, for example, wanted to know how they could serve. Within twenty-four hours, they had established a two-hundred-fifty drop telephone board in a building which <u>they</u> had picked as the most desirable for G.H.Q. in YOKOHAMA.

They established radio facilities so that our forces could communicate immediately with Washington. They turned over all of their available vehicles to our armed forces. They met our finance officers and offered whatever currency we should require--we did not even have to use our invasion currency. They continued to operate all of their governmental agencies for our benefit. The tourist bureau even beamed a broadcast to the United States extolling the beauties of JAPAN as a tourist paradise. They asked to examine General MacArthur's list of war criminals, and added a few names. There was not one single case of treachery or sabotage that I heard of. There was not one surly word spoken, or threat mumbled, or scowl on a face. In short, it was impossible to believe that only a few days before we had been fighting a deadly war against the world's most despicable people.

It was incredible to watch the GI invade JAPAN. At first, air-born troops ran wild, but soon this the first blush of victory was under control. As other troops arrived, the war was quickly forgotten. The GI's went on sight-seeing expeditions, shopping on the Ginza, talking to pedestrians, clamoured for the "geishas" who had been put out of business at the beginning of the war to work in manufacturing plants, they visited the DIET and stood with bared heads while interpreters exhibited the golden throne of the Emperor, the royal box and the diplomats corner in the House of Peers. One would have thought that they were in London. They bartered and traded in the stores, buying up everything in sight. They rode on electric trains and street cars packed in like sardines with the multitudes who were returning to the towns.

I talked to a great many people, reporters, scientists, soldiers, civilians I learned a few things which have not appeared in the papers. I learned how disgusted the army officers and newspaper correspondents are with the details of the surrender terms. I saw on the streets the effect the gendarmerie has on the people, and I learned how bitterly opposed our forces are to their being allowed to remain in power. I heard of our high command's list of forty-seven war criminals which included none of these ferocious, sadistic, brutal, treacherous people. I learned, with dismay, how well the clause concerning the occupation of military installations was working for the Japanese. I heard a scientist, a high ranking army officer heading a special mission to Japan, complain bitterly that he could not get the vital records that he so much wanted. Under the terms of the surrender, the American Forces were obliged not to occupy any Japanese Military installation until after the Japanese had completely evacuated them. My scientist acquaintance wanted these records, but he knew that if he asked for them in the prescribed manner, that would merely hasten their destruction by those in command of the laboratories. I heard another top-ranking army officer cursing the regulation which prescribed that they request Japanese soldiers for working parties through the foreigh office. I heard him curse the rule which forbade him to order Japanese troops stationed at the ATSUKA airfield to maintain the landing strips which were so rapidly going to pieces under the heavy loads of our planes. When this same officer requested labor through the foreign office, he was furnished five hundred korean laborers that the Japanese had imported for this work. The Koreans, it developed, were mere children from eight to fifteen years of age. Not a single Japanese soldier or worker was ordered out.

One of our correspondents told me that he had listened at length to a top-ranking Japanese scientist boasting that already his men were at work to discover the "super-atomic bomb," and nothing has been done about it.

As I traveled about the country-side, I was impressed at the unconcern of our forces. Rarely did I see a man, or officer, with a gun or side arm, and in truth, no one felt any danger. Peasants, while frightened at first, soon learned that we had no intention of killing them, and the children swarmed the roads laughing, waving, saluting, begging, playing, as in any country. I talked to a teacher of English in a small Japanese town, a man of seventy who had studied at San Francisco years before. He said that the people of Japan didn't want to fight. He said that the Emperor didn't want the war, but that the Peers and war lords had insisted. He said that the people were so accustomed to obedience that it was impossible for them to do anything but follow their leaders. Now that peace has been declared and their leaders had ordered them to return to peaceful pursuits and treat the American Forces with respect, they were only too happy to do so. I talked to a street peddlar with a few pitiful wares who said that he had not suffered too much. He merely wanted for "booze and sugar". I talked to a chemical engineer who boasted that their industry was at least seventy percent intact and that they would be competing for world trade before we knew it.

On the other hand, I was heartened to visit a commander of our naval facilities who took delight in telling us how he, the Navy, was handling the situation. Four of the Japanese admirals are his messenger boys. They sit in the orderly room on the ground floor of the naval headquarters and come when he rings for them. One acts as the dock master and was charged with getting the damaged dry-docks back into commission. Already he and his forces have put four of the five back in working order and are completely manning them. The others he uses for various duties. For example, one of the Japanese banks was exchanging American dollars at the rate of four yen to the dollar, which was the pre-war rate, instead of the presently established rate of fifteen to the dollar. The commander promptly closed the bank. The chief of police was acting surly and refused to salute our forces, and the commander required one of his admiral messengers to lock up the police chief in a U. S. Navy brig. When the commander wants something done, he ignored the foreign office and orders Japanese labor to be produced directly from the naval forces quartered in the Navy Yard. He was outspoken in his criticisms of G.H.Q.'s handling of the situation and in fact was broadcasting his views to the United States when he received a message to the effect that G.H.Q. was "sick and tired of people saying that they are handling the Japanese with "kid gloves". No, the commander wasn't letting them have their own way, not for one moment. I wish there were many more like him in high places there.

No doubt, I should not comment on the situation as I have, not having the whole picture and merely relying on my eyes and ears for my reactions, but as an American, I am used to using my eyes and listening, and drawing my own conclusions from what I see. To be sure, the army is correcting some of its practices. Personally, I am afraid that whatever they do will be "too little and too late". I fear the Japs already have the laugh on us, and that within twenty or twenty-five years, they will be back again a wiser and stronger foe.

Index

to

a series of interviews

with

Captain Willard G. Triest

CEC, USNR (Ret.)

ADONE, Charles: leading designer with Standard Oil of New Jersey, p. 19;
         Triest enlists his aid with plans for BOBCAT project,
         p. 23; p. 36;

AMERICAN RED CROSS: p. 71; in charge of the R and R program in New Zealand,
         p. 119 ff;

ASCENSION ISLAND: building of base - WWII - p. 46;

BISSETT, Captain Andrew: Commanding Officer, Seabees stationed on Espiritu
         Santo, p. 64-65; p. 84; p. 87; sends Triest up to Tulagi to
         take over 27th Battalion, p. 90; p. 104; regimental Commander
         in Okinawa, p. 186; p. 190;

SS BRAZIL: two battalions of Seabees depart from San Francisco for Espiritu Santo,
         p. 61;

BUREAU OF YARDS AND DOCKS - Navy Department: p. 5; p. 18; urgent need for
         advance base on Christmas Island - fueling station enroute
         to Australia, p. 21; p. 37-8; failure to get more than 1-A
         priority, p. 38;

CABANISS, Lt. Wm. F.E.: Executive Officer, 27th Battalion, Seabees, p. 92;
         goes with Triest to Japan, p. 213; goes with Triest to Korea,
         p. 220-28;

CHAPLAIN: role of the chaplain with the 27th Battalion of Seabees, p. 146-7;

CONSTRUCTION DETACHMENT: the first one (WWII) (later SEABEES) organized for
         the BOBCAT project, p. 24 ff; p. 39-40; p. 44; see entries:
              57th Construction Battalion
              27th Battalion, Seabees

DUDDLESTON, Shorty: recruited from Standard Oil of New Jersey to supervise
         construction job on Christmas Island, p. 27-8; his call
         on Admirals King and Moreell, p. 29-30; put in uniform within
         one day, p. 31 ff; p. 44;

EMIRAU: p. 127; the 27th Battalion builds an airfield, port, etc. p. 127 ff;
         p. 135; a rifle range to improve marksmanship, p. 144;
         a chapel, p. 144;

ESPIRITU SANTO: 57th Battalion arrives in Segund Channel - told of delay in
         unloading, p. 63; recreation, p. 80-2; p. 100; see entries:
         Fifty-seventh Construction Battalion;

FIFTY-SEVENTH CONSTRUCTION BATTALION: Triest becomes Executive Officer,
         p. 47; training during construction on the Gulfport Base,
         p. 57; they off-load at Espiritu Santo, p. 64 ff; task
         they performed on Espiritu Santo, p. 67-8; building a
         degaussing station, p. 74; building a new type bridge,
         p. 84 ff;

FINNEY, Cap: of Standard Oil, New Jersey - in charge of pipelines and tank
         farms, p. 16; p. 19; p. 27;

GEORGE A. FULLER CONSTRUCTION CO.: p. 11-12; p. 14-15; p. 16-17; p. 23;

GUADALCANAL: p.73; p. 79; p. 91-2; p. 100; the big storm washes away the Nalimbu River Bridge, p. 110; task of building a pontoon bridge, p. 110 ff; p. 132; the natives and the giant can opener, p. 133-4;

HARDMAN, Lt. Cdr. Dwight P.: Commanding Officer of 57th Construction Battalion, p. 63; p. 90;

HAWAII: five day stopover in Hawaii enroute to Okinawa - opportunity for acquiring other needed supplies, p. 183-5;

HUNTINGTON, Capt. Everett: Bureau of Yards and Docks, p. 20; p. 29; p. 31;

ICELAND: work on bases there prior to December, 1941, p. 12-13; Triest not satisfied with progress under Geo. Fuller Construction Co. and Merrit, Chapman and Scott, p. 13 ff; Triest goes to Standard Oil of New Jersey for design work, p. 16 ff;

JUNGLE ROT: p. 140;

KAUFFMAN, VADM James Laurence: Commanding Officer, base in Iceland (WWII), p.

KESSING, RADM Oliver O.(Scrappy): Commanding Officer Naval Base, Tulagi, p. 10

KING, Fleet Admiral Ernest: his reception of Duddleston for the Christmas Isla project, p. 30-31;

KOREA: Triest and his executive officer fly to Korea for a visit, p. 220.

MALARIA: the necessity for combatting malaria, p. 139-40;

MEAT ON THE TABLE: title of the history of the 27th Battalion, Seabees, p. 165 ff; the private publishing effort, p. 168-9;

MERRITT, CHAPMAN AND SCOTT: p. 11-12; p. 14; p. 16; design work contract cancelled but construction contract UK and Iceland bases continued p. 17; p. 23;

MILLER, Capt. Raymond V.(CEC-USN(Ret.)): in charge of construction, Quonset Pt., RI p. 8; p. 13; p. 17;

MOREELL, Admiral Ben: p. 5; p. 18; p. 25; p. 29-30; he speeds the process to g Duddleston in uniform in one day - for Christmas Island job, p. ff; gets privilege of reassigning men to proper categories upon entering the SeaBees, p. 58; p. 169;

NCTC - Davisville, R.I.: construction camp for Seabees on east coast, p. 47; Triest assigned as Executive Officer, 57th Construction Battalion, p. 47; the mock enemy attack on the base - arranged by Triest, p. 49-57; p. 67; p. 70;

NEW ZEALAND: the 27th Battalion goes to New Zealand for month of R and R, p. 118 ff; p. 126; p. 164;

OKINAWA: destination of the 27th Battalion after stay at Camp Parks, p. 181 ff; getting settled, p. 188-9; the 27th Battalion constructs Route 1 from Naha to the south, also a supply depot - in addition quarters for the natives in the NE sector, p. 191-2; use of DDT in eliminating flies, p. 195; the effects of a big typhoon, p. 216 ff;

OPERATION BOBCAT: fueling base on Christmas Island - story of this urgent project, p. 21-44; the first construction detachment in uniform, p. 24; old Hollywood movie, TABU viewed for ideas on terrain, p. 25; recruitment of necessary officers to build base, p. 26 ff; need for a welder, p. 39-40; convoy of 400 trucks from Quonset Pt. to Charleston in order to catch sailing of two merchant ships for Boro-boro, p. 41-2;

PAINTER, Capt. Bill: a civil engineer who made initial surveys of a great number of Pacific islands prior to troop landings, p. 127 ff;

PONTOONS: use of pontoons by the SeaBees, p. 138-9; see also entries:
                                       GUADALCANAL
                                       TULAGI

POTSDAM AGREEMENT: its unfortunate results as they pertained to Korea, p. 222-233;

QUONSET POINT, R.I.: first tour of duty, p. 5; p. 7-9; Triest becomes budget officer, p. 10-11; see also entries: Operation BOBCAT
                                                              NCTC Davisville

ROOSEVELT, Eleanor (Mrs. Franklin D.): her visit to Espiritu Santo, p. 80;

RYUKYUANS: natives of Okinawa. See entries under OKINAWA; Seabees provide facilities for 240,000 people, p. 200-12; customs, sanitation, etc. p. 218-9;

SCHEFFLEIN, Jay: Commanding Officer, AVS school at Quonset Point, p. 9-10;

SCUTTLEBUT: a poem - role of scuttlebut in life of the Seabee Camp, p. 152-3;

SEABEES: re-classification of men upon entering the Seabees - an arrangement of Admiral Moreell and the BuPers, p. 58-60;

STRAUSS, RADM Lewis: p. 6;

TOKYO: Triest and his executive officer visit Japan on the second day of the occupation, p. 213-5;

TRIEST, Captain Willard G., CEC, USNR (Ret.): personal data, p. 1-5;

TRUK: p. 135;

TULAGI: p. 73; Triest arrives to take command of the 27th Battalion, p. 92; building of the first tank farm, p. 94; account of some exploits on Tulagi before Triest came to command, p. 106-8; p. 132;

TWENTY-SEVENTH BATTALION - SEABEES: Triest takes over command on Tulagi, p. 92 ff; his first meeting with the men, p. 96-8; their previous record of repairs on 450 ships in a period of a year, p. 100-2; Triest moves Battalion to Guadalcanal and construction of a sanitary camp, 103-4; Battalion ordered to Auckland, New Zealand for a month of R and R, p. 104 ff; they build a pontoon bridge over the Nalimbu River on Guadalcanal, p. 111-117; Triest comments on the flow of supplies from the States, p. 136-7; Triest on the varied talents of his men - their ingenuity, p. 148-9; past-time pursuits, p. 154-5; enroute home p. 156 ff; trip back to States affords Triest opportunity to compile a history of the Battalion in the South Pacific, p. 159 ff; Camp Parks outside of San Francisco, p. 164; a free lance writer is engaged to work on the history, p. 165 ff; preparation at Camp Parks for duty on Okinawa, p. 169-80; overhaul and submission of their needed complement of equipment, p. 173-4; the new dentist chair, p. 174 ff; on to Okinawa, p. 181 ff; they take advantage of stop-over in Hawaii to gather needed supplies, p. 182-3;

UNITED KINGDOM - bases WWII: p. 12 ff;

USO - provides entertainment for troops in the South Pacific, p. 130;

van LEER, Lt. Comdr. Wayne: p. 17-18; p. 29;